History Soup
Stories of Oswego's Past

Nancy Dunis

History Soup Press

©2022 Nancy Dunis

ISBN: 9798846128613

All rights reserved. Thank you in advance for respecting the author's rights. Uploading or distributing photos, scans or any content from this book without prior consent is theft of the author's intellectual property. For permission requests, please contact the author at: nancy@thehistoricconnection.com

Cover photo: is one Lake Oswego Review photojournalist Beth Ryan shot of her Sunny HIll farm off Stafford Road. This is one of the 700 photographs in the Lake Oswego Public Library's Beth Ryan Collection.

Unless otherwise noted, the photos in this book are from the Lake Oswego Public Library (LOPL) Digital History Collection.

Several photographs in the book of early Oswego Lake were taken in the early 1900s by William Bickner, one of Joseph and Vctoria Bickner's seven children. William died in 1931 when his car skidded off the road In loose gravel and flipped over twice.

Independently published by History Soup Press

Book design: Becky Luening Book Arts

This book is dedicated to Mary Puskas, Oswego Heritage Council Board President 2022; Gary Stein, former Lake Oswego Review *Editor; and Bill Warner, Oswego Heritage Council Director Emeritus.*

"Growing up in beautiful Oswego—
out of doors, in the fields and on the streams—
gave me a fine, wholesome early life, which
has been of great value to me ever since."

General Nathan F. Twining, USAF
Chairman, Joint Chiefs of Staff

Table of Contents

Foreword by Gary Stein ix
Acknowledgements xi
The Wheels on the Bus Go 'round and 'round xiii

Welcome to History Soup 1

FIRST STOP: Oswego's First Inhabitants
    Early Native American Influence 7

SECOND STOP: Nancy Writes (A–L)
    Bickner Brothers Form Orchestra 13
    Ladies Man, Woodsman, Best Speller 17
    Oswego's First Librarian 20
    Named for Daniel or Alphonse? 23
    A Pear Tree, a Plaque, a School 26
    Surgeon, Physician, Musician 33
    Shipley-Cook Farmstead 37
    Cook Connection to Quilts Dates Back 100 Years 42
    Savior of the Sequoia 46
    An Island in Oswego Lake? 51
    Flames Could Be Seen from Afar 53
    Fanning the Flames of History 57
    Murder in Lake Oswego? 60
    A Grande Dame Was She in 1893 62
    Lake Oswego Residents Remember Lakewood School 67
    Kitchen Counter Drive Saves Tryon 69
    Rare Plants Were Her Bailiwick 71

THIRD STOP: Nancy Writes (M–Z)

Always Ready for a Fire..........................77
"Singin' in the Rain" 80
Lover of Trees 82
Men of Power 86
Live Where You Play 89
A Flavorite Spot................................. 93
Cementing Portland's Future 97
Dig, Dug, Done 101
Oswego Heritage House & Museum 104
A Plot with a View.............................. 111
Guardian Angel of Oswego Pioneer Cemetery..........114
Electricity Comes to Town 117
The First Ore Mined in Oswego 121
Yes, Virginia, Linus Pauling Spent Time in Oswego 124
A *Leafing* Legacy 126
I Married a Taxidermist 129
Postmistresses and Postmaster 132
Mary Got the Mines.... Did Henry Get the Shaft?.......134
To Market, to Market...........................138
A Talented Presswoman........................142
The House that John Built 145
Art Under Cover Uncovered 149
Birdwatching in the Northwest 152
Chairman Joint Chiefs of Staff 155
Wallings Leave a Legacy of Fruit and Education........158

FOURTH STOP: On the Water

    Lake Grove Swim Park..165

    Willa Wows 'em on Water...............................167

    Never Tell an Ex–PT Boater It Can't Be Done..........170

    Eyes in the Back of His Head.......................174

FIFTH STOP: Oswego—Fun, Facts, Firsts

    Who's In a Name?...179

    Lake Oswego Firsts...184

SIXTH STOP: Through History We Connect

    HistoryConnection Red Carpet Club..................190

    Connect with Nancy.......................................189

LUNCH STOP: Gazpacho Soup Recipe

    Nancy's second favorite soup........................193

LAST STOP: Resources and Credits 195

About the Author...198

Index..200

Foreword

During my tenure as editor of the *Lake Oswego Review*, Nancy Dunis wrote a monthly column about the history of Lake Oswego and surrounding communities. She conceived all of the story ideas, did all of the research, and then wrote about everything from a favorite old-time ice cream shop and World War II–era PT boat to the power plant on Oswego Lake. Her use of details and her ability to connect the dots between people and places brought history alive and made it relevant to a whole new generation of readers.

Nancy's versatility as a writer also allowed her to take on other writing assignments: publishing a newsletter for the City of Lake Oswego and publishing her own *HistoryConnection* newzine.

As the Lake Oswego School District prepared to tear down Lakeridge Junior High, Nancy became the *Review's* lead reporter on the project. She explained the central role the school had played in the city and in the lives of so many Lake Oswegans. She told the story of handcrafted tiles that graced the walls of the school, and let folks know how they could preserve their own piece of history. In print and online, Nancy became the go-to source for news and information about a very beloved institution. These are just a few examples of her ability to tell stories and connect with readers.

There is a folksy feel and an underlying sense of humor to everything Nancy writes, making it almost seem as if she is sitting around a table with a bunch of friends and sharing favorite tales. That's a rare gift, and one I'm glad to have witnessed during my time at the *Review*. If you're looking for a consummate storyteller and writing pro, there's no one I could recommend more highly than Nancy Dunis.

—Gary M. Stein

Ackowledgements

THE MAKING OF *HISTORY SOUP* is a story in itself, and though I would be hard pressed to name everyone in the community who contributed to my History Connections columns, I want to acknowledge a few key individuals who provided the encouragement, guidance, and friendship that made this endeavor not only possible but especially rewarding for me, the writer.

Bill Warner—history buff and avid reader of my History Connection column: You were one of the first to read my column and you read it regularly. Thank you.

Dee Denton—admired community leader: You would be delighted to know I'm starting on that festival backstory book we talked about. Wish you were here.

Gary Stein—former editor of the *Lake Oswego Review* who greenlighted 98 percent of my historical content ideas: Thanks for your guidance and leadership with the 2 percent you redlighted.

Rick Cook—stalwart steward of our community's historical resources with whom History Connections resonated: Thank you for the inspiring content ideas.

Jim Rathbun—neighbor, classmate, faithful reader of my column: I loved your email reminiscences to me about growing up in LO. I miss you, my friend.

Becky Luening—for her patience and graphic design skills in pulling this book together.

Special Tribute to Bill Warner

Bill, whenever I ran into you around town, you always commented positively about one of my articles you'd just read. That meant a lot coming from a man who knew more about Lake Oswego history than I'd ever hope to know.

I think of you every time I drive by the historic rose garden at the Oswego Heritage House and Museum and don't see that eyesore of a "white arbor" protruding upwards in the landscape, looking very much out of place. You didn't think it belonged there in the first place—you were right—but the executive director at the time thought it would entice couples to rent the rose garden for their wedding because it was such a romantic setting.

I wonder how many couples got married under that arbor… such a beautiful view looking down A Avenue at the cars, trucks, buses and surrounded by continual traffic noise on the north and south sides of the garden.

—*Nancy Dunis*

The Wheels on the Bus Go 'round and 'round...

B<small>Y PURCHASING THIS BOOK,</small> you have automatically been assigned a seat on "Gus the Bus," a vintage 1945 Chevy school bus headed down history lane in Oswego, Oregon.

History Soup is a collection of articles about Lake Oswego history I wrote under my own byline for the *Lake Oswego Review* titled "History Connection." The column started in 2013 and appeared monthly for five years through 2018.

History Connection morphed into an online digital publication I refer to as a newzine—combination newsletter and magazine—in 2021. It features biographical sketches of the men (HIStories) and women (HERstories) who shaped Oswego; historical resources I have found useful; interesting and unique historical books I've come across; the Oswego trivia challenge, history quotes, and more. To subscribe to the HistoryConnection: visit www.thehistoricconnection.com or email nancy@thehistoricconnection.com

Many of the articles in this book have been updated and enhanced for clarity and reading ease. However, since the subject matter is Oswego's history I chose to use words as they would have been used historically (i.e., Lake Oswego referred to as Oswego or Oswego Lake). I have tried to keep the language the same as it was originally written or referred to, unless it was confusing or offensive.

Glancing at the table of contents, you'll notice it is organized as if you were going on a tour. You *are* going on a tour—a virtual one. Stop One is early Oswego history. Stops Two and Three are collections of my articles organized alphabetically by subject—A–L and M–Z respectively.

A ride back in time

Before I rev up the engine to start the tour, a few words about "Gus the Bus":

"It's not in bad shape and for the most part, intact... a few rusted out areas, several broken windows, some dents and scratches, and in desperate need of a paint job," Sean Kennedy remembers thinking when he saw the vintage 1945 Chevy school bus. He bought the bus in 2011.

After five years of blood, sweat, tears—and a small fire—Kennedy brought the bus back to life as you see it today. He replaced the original Chevy bus's old running gear with more current Dodge D35 and installed a Cummins diesel engine for reliability. He comments, "The bus remained in Twin Falls during the five-and-a-half years of restoration. I would travel

xv

to Twin Falls and stay there for two months at a time working on the bus with Will Ruby, owner of Dream Ride Builders. He is absolutely the best when it comes to restoring and rebuilding vintage vehicles.

"My color scheme for the bus was inspired by the Glacier and Yellowstone National Parks buses from the early '40s and the historic Bedford OB buses in England. Bedford OB was a type of bus chassis manufactured by the Bedford Company in 1939. I wanted an 'Eddie Bauer meets National Parks' look and feel. The various shades of green and the creme color of the exterior combined with the earth-tone stripes of the upholstered seats fit the look I wanted."

Prior to Kennedy's purchase of the bus, a private party in Hagerman, Idaho, bought the bus in 1959 from the Gooding, Idaho, School District, turning it into a funky family camper; then used it as a workshop and storage receptacle. For several years Gus sat parked, neglected and unused.

Built by the Wayne Corporation based in Richmond, Indiana, the 1945 Chevy school bus was one of only 600 manufactured that year. Wayne Corporation's predecessor, Wayne Works, founded in 1837, produced the first so-called "school bus" in 1914 by combining a "kid hack" wagon body with an automotive chassis. A "kid hack" is a horse-drawn wagon used to transport several children at one time.

Bus designs in the early years were much different than they are today. Passengers entered and exited through a door at the rear—a design begun in non-motorized days to void startling horses—and they sat facing the sides, not forward like today's buses.

Well known for its many design innovations, Wayne Corporation became a leading manufacturer of buses. The company produced the first guardrails used on the sides of all school buses and introduced the first bus design known as "The Wayne Busette." This design featured a cutaway van chassis, meaning a van-type front end with a cab. The cutaway van chassis remains one of the most popular bus design features today.

Wayne's crowning achievement was the Wayne Lifeguard structural safety design, introduced in 1973, which featured continuous interior and exterior longitudinal panels. The Lifeguard's design helped pave the way for the all-important U.S. Federal Motor Vehicle Safety Standards for school buses.

For more information about the Vintage Tour Bus Company's events, tours and whatnot, visit https://vintagetourbus.com.

Welcome to History Soup

IF YOU ARE READING THIS, thank you for picking up the book. May the content inspire you to explore more. Maybe you will discover a story about Oswego's past that you never knew ... or have an "Aha!" moment when you personally connect with history. The book may be a walk down memory lane for you, evoking thoughts, feelings, and memories about the past. All of the aforementioned were my objectives in compiling the stories of Oswego's past for *History Soup*.

Title tale

History Soup seemed like the perfect title for this book because it lets the reader know there's a connection to my first book, *Story Soup*, a collection of humorous anecdotes from my life experience, which I wrote as part of the "Jottings from 5th and G" writing group.

Like *Story Soup*, *History Soup* is a collection of articles I wrote under my own byline for the *Lake Oswego Review* from 2013 until 2018. The column was called "History Connection." The content has been changed to protect the guilty.

HISTORY CONNECTION
Nancy Dunis

Here's the backstory about how I derived the *Story Soup* title. *Chicken Soup for the Soul* intrigued and inspired me, especially the soup part. What is soup but a number of ingredients combined to create a delectable taste or sought-after outcome?

Perfect. I wanted soup in the title because the book combines articles I'd written over a period of time; but the word soup by itself didn't sound very appetizing.

An epiphany struck in the middle of the night. You know ... the kind where you're jolted from prone to upright, wishing you had something to write with and write on so you could jot down the idea. Lord knows I would never remember it in the morning. I now keep pen and paper on the bed next to me for these epiphanic—is that a word?—moments. It was so obvious, I had missed it: *Story Soup*. Why not? These were stories combined together—like a soup—for the enjoyment of readers.

The title of this book likewise jumped into my brain. *Wham!* It made sense: the historical snippets coming together created another wonderful soup, *History Soup!* The recipe would be similar to *Story Soup,* but with different ingredients.

Why this book?

I have always enjoyed writing. I loved writing research papers in college. That's a far cry from this kind of writing, but it's writing just the same. Not only did I enjoy writing the papers—and my masters thesis—but I thrived on doing research. I can lose myself for hours in facts, tidbits, backstories. I have that one-thing-leads-to-another and I-can't-remember-where-I-started syndrome. (I wish there was a vaccine for that.)

The first History Connection article I wrote in 2013 was entitled "History Connection connects the dots." The last article, in 2018, focused on *Lake Oswego Review* staff photojournalist Beth Ryan. Although I clipped and saved every History Connection article I wrote, I wanted something more permanent than a pile of newspaper clippings filed away somewhere. I wanted something I could pass down to family and friends—and I wanted a memoir for myself. Putting my articles into a book format was the perfect answer. Two years passed from the time I decided to do a book until I got serious about getting it done. As much as I'd always wanted to write a book, I had no idea about the amount of time it would take. I really had to commit myself to staying focused—a big lesson I had forgotten when I retired. But here it is.

What's next?

More books, of course.... I launched a publishing company in 2021 called History Soup Press which publishes my mini newzine the *HistoriConnection*. I'm planning to publish an eBook series about the history of Lake Grove, a series about Oswego's pioneer families, and a "Getting to Know Your Neighborhood" gazette for people new to Lake Oswego. The HistoryConnection Red Carpet Club is in the works. This is a membership-based community for history enthusiasts, offering exclusive content, tours, workshops and lectures.

Follow me on social media or visit my websites to find more details about the HistoryConnection Red Carpet Club, to purchase books, or to share your own ideas and experiences.

Facebook: @historyconnections-oregon
(*You need to join the group.*)

Website: https://thehistoricconnection.com

FIRST STOP
Oswego's First Inhabitants

LAKE OSWEGO PUBLIC LIBRARY DIGITAL HISTORY COLLECTION
PHOTO BY WILL BICKNER

"And they called the lake Waluga because when the Indians said 'Wah–loo–ga' it sounded like the cry of wild swans."

—Lucia Bliss, Oswego's first librarian

Early Native American Influence

WHILE SORTING THROUGH SOME FILES at the Oswego Heritage House, Candee Clark Jones, then–board president of the Oswego Heritage Council, discovered this essay written by Dorothy Thurlow titled "Indians of Oswego." Jones forwarded the essay to me, suggesting it might be a great article for my History Connection column. I agreed; did a bit of editing and submitted it. The article appeared in September 2015.

Since Oswego history dates back to the Native Americans who inhabited this area before the early pioneers flocked west to stake their donation land claims, this article seemed like a perfect beginning for *History Soup.*

Prior to 1828, there were about 100,000 Native Americans in Oregon. Between 1826 and 1845, measles, scarlet fever and small pox afflicted the Indians. White men fur traders, sailors and early pioneers carried these diseases, infecting the tribes as they interacted with them. By 1845, approximately 80,000 had died, leaving about 20,000 in Oregon. Lewis and Clark wrote that in 1806 only 800 members of the Clackamas Tribe remained. In 1851 there were 88.

Early settlers remember a Native American village across the Willamette River where Jennings Lodge is. The denizens of this village lived almost the same way as their ancestors, hunting, trapping, and fishing at Willamette Falls in Oregon City. Those who fished—and there were many when the salmon were running—sold a 35- or 40-pound salmon to the settlers for

Native American meeting place on Diamond Head.
OREGON HISTORICAL SOCIETY PHOTO COLLECTION

50 cents. Often a Native American would carry a fish on his back a mile or more to deliver it to a pioneer's home. When they weren't salmon fishing or hunting, many could be seen paddling their dugout canoes up and down the Willamette.

Women of the tribes gathered plants for food; prepared meals; wove baskets of all different sorts and sizes for various uses; beheaded, filleted, skinned, and cooked the salmon; and did the washing. Frequently the pioneers hired the women to do their washing, paying them 50 cents for a week's wash.

As the tribes moved about on land, they created footpaths, which eventually widened into trails to accommodate horses and oxen and wagons. Eventually the trails widened even more, resulting in dirt roads, which then became gravel roads and finally paved roads. Many of the roads we use today started out as narrow footpaths. Stafford Road, known in the early days as Market Road, and Rosemont Road are two examples. The early Market Road went north and south from the Tualatin River to Portland; Rosemont Road led from the Willamette River west at Linn City to Market Road.

Other footpaths led to two bluffs that towered above the lake—Council Bluff on the north side and Phantom Bluff on the south. Phantom Bluff is just off South Shore Road; Council Bluff—now known as Diamond Head—is on the north side of the lake at the end of North Shore Road. Various tribes from the valley gathered at these spots around the council fires for trading, storytelling, games, dancing, and tribal meetings.

Arrowheads found on Crazy Man's Island (later Jantzen Island/Halvorson Island)—a steep drop into the lake below Diamond Head—suggest that young Native American boys probably met there for swimming, fishing, hunting, and canoeing.

These early Native Americans named the lake "Waluga" because when they said "wah—loo—gah," it sounded like an imitation of the cry of the wild swan.

NOTE: In Dorothy Thurlow's original article, written in the 1950s, she refers to Native Americans as "Indians," a term not likely to be found in essays today, and I have changed the wording to bring the article up to date. Much of Dorothy's information came from Lucia Bliss' manuscript, "Early History of Oswego, Oregon," and *Oregon's Iron Dream* by Mary Goodall. Dorothy and Don Thurlow lived next door to Candee on Tenth Street in First Addition when she was growing up.

SECOND STOP
NancyWrites (A–L)

"The more you know of your history, the more liberated you are."

—Maya Angelou

Bickner Brothers Form Orchestra

JOSEPH W. BICKNER, SR., and his wife Victoria, both born in Prague, came to Oregon from Minnesota in the 1880s. The family settled with Victoria's sister and brother-in-law; Clara and Henry Gans, who owned the general store in South Town located near what is now McVey Avenue and Erickson Street (near Grimm's corner). Joseph Bickner, Sr., bought the general store and living quarters—all one building—from Gans in about 1892. The Bickner family, consisting of five sons and two daughters—Mary A., Joseph Jr., Henry B., William E., John, Lillian, Charles—all helped run the store.

In 1903 Joseph, Sr., and three of his sons—John, William, and Charles—bought an old hotel in "New Town" located on State Street between A and B Avenues south of the Texaco station. They remodeled it, making it a general merchandise store, J. Bickner & Sons. (For a short time the Bickner family owned two stores.)

The lower level of J. Bickner & Sons contained groceries and dry goods; the balcony contained hardware. To the rear was a barn for three horses, two delivery wagons, and a hayloft. The front of the building, one level, was used to store grain and supplies and also housed the refrigerators. Some years later a walk-in refrigerator was installed so that both Bickner & Sons and Bethke's Meat Market next door could use it.

Joseph Bickner, Sr., died in 1921 at age 78, but the Bickner brothers kept the store going until Safeway purchased the building in 1938. In the years that followed, Safeway moved out of the building; Freda Bain opened a dress shop, which was replaced by Lucille's—another dress shop. The Tates, owners of Tim's Germs, purchased the building from the proprietor of Lucille's and operated their jewelry store upstairs in the building. They leased the street level area to Imperial Flowers and Heads Up Stylists. According to Tim and Nadeen Tate, the adjoining section of the building housed an auto parts store.

Selling groceries and making music

Although the Bickners as a family played a major role in Oswego's commerce in the early 1900s, the individual offspring of Joseph, Sr., and Victoria also made their own significant contributions.

Mary, the oldest, taught school at the Grange Hall; was a principal at Oswego School; and accompanied the church choir on the piano.

Joe, one of the brothers, co-owned J. Bickner & Sons General Store on State Street. When the store was sold to Safeway in 1938, Joe retired to pursue his interest in gold mining. He married Carrie Wells.

William, another co-owner of J. Bickner & Sons, died in a tragic automobile accident near McMinnville when his car skidded in loose gravel and flipped—twice. He married Edna Kingkade. Mrs. Bickner taught 3rd and 4th grade in Oswego's Grange Hall and she led the drive to organize the Congregational Church located at 4th and D where the library is now. Will and Edna lived at the corner of 2nd and B (where Kienow's was in 1985).

John, also a co-owner of J. Bickner & Sons, married Pearl Nida. He built their home on the two lots just north of the store in 1903. Originally the house faced State Street, but in 1938 John repositioned it to face B Avenue. John also built the Texaco station at the front of the two lots on State Street. He was the second mayor of Oswego and also president of Oswego State Bank.

Lillian, second youngest of the seven children, taught music for several years and was active in community affairs as a charter member and past matron of the Waluga chapter of the Order of the Eastern Star and past noble grand of Dena Rebekah Lodge. She lived on Evergreen Street; loved canoeing on the lake as much as she loved music. Lillian never married.

Charles married Marie Jarisch in 1916. After the store was sold, he and his family moved to Florida. Marie passed away in 1945. After her death, Charles married Agda Benson.

All five of the "Bickner Boys" taught themselves to play musical instruments and formed Oswego's first family Orchestra (see photo on page 11). Sisters Mary and Lillian played the piano. Lillian accompanied the Bickner Boys orchestra; Mary accompanied the church choir. It's not clear if they were self-taught like their brothers.

Ladies Man, Woodsman, Best Speller

Caleb Barnes, one of the first donation land claimants to homestead the rugged, hilly, densely-forested west end of Oswego Lake, acquired his property in 1851. Born in 1818, census records show that Barnes hailed from Canada, arriving in Oregon in 1848 when he was 33. The Bryant land claim butted up to Barnes' to the south; Prosser's claim was to the north.

LAKE OSWEGO PUBLIC LIBRARY DIGITAL HISTORY COLLECTION
PHOTO BY WILL BICKNER

Little has been written about Caleb Barnes: his reasons for coming to Oregon; what he did for a living prior to his arrival here; when he died; where he is buried. It is interesting to speculate that since he was Canadian, he might have come to the Oregon Territory as an employee of the Hudson's Bay Company. Upon his arrival in Oregon, records show he lived for a time in Linn City, founded by Major Robert Moore—a colleague of Dr. John McLoughlin. Dr. McLoughlin founded Oregon City. Major Robert Moore founded Robin's Nest, which became Linn city, then later West Linn.

Barnes built his dwelling in a forest amidst dogwoods, maples, and alder trees on rocky terrain overlooking the lake. When deciding where to situate his house, closer to the road or having a view of the pristine lake, he chose close to the road. It was more practical for transportation purposes.

Although he was a bachelor, Barnes rarely experienced loneliness. The road from Tualatin Plains to Oregon City cut through his property, which meant there were always folks traveling back and forth. Plus he had his horse and his boat to carry him to Oswego whenever he wanted to socialize. He took part in many "spell downs" at the Grange Hall, earning the reputation as the best speller in the county.

Parties of campers would often disturb his wilderness-like living when they came to the lake in their wagons for a vacation of catfishing. The shores of Oswego Lake remained pristine and quiet, the only disruption of the water being a log tow. The harbinger of the development of Lake Grove, Caleb Barnes' single dwelling inspired several other pioneer families of the late 1840s and early '50s to file donation land claims, including Carman, Brown, Prosser, Bryant, and Draper.

Oregon Iron and Steel (OIS) owned a great deal of property around Oswego Lake. When those properties went on the market in 1912, the area around Barnes' homestead began developing. Lake Grove, platted in 1912, was named by OIS for its proximity to the lake and groves of trees as far as the eye could see.

Owners of Owego Pipe Foundry cleared the land because they needed trees to burn for charcoal to fuel the foundry. According to *Oregon's Iron Dream* by Mary Goodall, Caleb Barnes was a woodsman (a person who worked in the woods.) This leads me to think he might have been one of several workers who felled the trees.

By 1916, several houses were built on the lake and the acreage above the lake. There were quite a few houses built on Reese Road. Only a few houses, maybe three or four, were built on Boones Ferry, even though it was considered the main road. However, people didn't have automobiles then and traveled by the Red Electric. They wanted to live within proximity to the Lake Grove depot, meaning within walking distance of two or three blocks. The center of Lake Grove then was from Upper Drive to Reese Road.

Oswego's First Librarian

Born in Posen, Germany, Lucia Adelheide Bethke and her parents, Mr. and Mrs. Herman Bethke, immigrated to the United States in 1892, settling in Oswego. Lucia attended school at the Grange Hall when she was 14. (The Grange Hall would later become the American Legion building. After the Columbus Day storm of 1962 rendered the building unsafe, it was torn down.)

Lucia took her first teacher's exam in 1895 at age 17. Passing the exam entitled her to teach one year. Her first teaching job started in the fall of 1895 at Stafford School. Every day she drove a horse and buggy from Oswego to the school. She took her second teacher's exam in the spring of 1896, which entitled her to teach for two years. In 1896 and 1897 she taught in a two-room school in Clackamas, living with a local family there. Friday afternoons she would walk through the woods to the Willamette River, where a rowboat would take her across to Oswego to spend the weekend with her family. Sunday afternoons the rowboat ferried her back across the river to Clackamas.

Lucia Bethke Bliss

Donated books comprised first library

For years, members of the Oswego Women's Club talked about the need for library in Oswego, and created their own in 1914. When the Lake Oswego Library formed in 1924 as the Oswego Library Association, it was a volunteer organization comprised of donated books—about 100 volumes. Having married Ben Bliss in 1914, Lucia Bethke Bliss became its first volunteer. Her job ... cataloguing books. Circulation her first Saturday evening on the job was 28 books. So she could catalogue books efficiently and systematically, Bliss went to Portland to learn the Dewey decimal system. She also attended sessions in Salem to learn how to mend books.

Three years after her volunteer position as a cataloguer, Bliss became a part-time salaried librarian appointed by the City of Oswego, earning $15 a month. The library served the community three evenings a week and Saturday afternoons. In addition to her duties as a librarian, Mrs. Bliss collected money for water bills.

Bliss became the secretary of the first Clackamas County Library Committee in 1936. The following April the Clackamas County Library Association was organized.

She also instigated the travelling library. Using her own car, and paying for her own gas, she hauled boxes of books from the main library in Oregon City to Canby, Estacada, Clackamas, and Lake Oswego. At each stop, she would drop off boxes of new books and pick up those left the week before. Some of these "book stations" were in private homes. None of the aforementioned cities had "libraries" as such until she aroused an interest in books and reading.

Lucia Bethke Bliss is considered one of Oswego's first historians, certainly the first to document Oswego history. In 1944 she wrote a manuscript titled "The Foundation: Early History of Oswego, Oregon." Lake Oswego Public Library has a copy of the original manuscript.

In 1961, the Lake Oswego School District mimeographed the document so more copies could be made available to the public. The school district also published a hard copy which the library also has. Bliss' manuscript inspired Mary Goodall's book, *Oregon's Iron Dream,* published in 1958.

By 1945, circulation of books had increased to the point where Bliss needed an assistant. The late Mrs. Mary Strachan filled that role. When Lucia Bethke Bliss retired on July 1, 1947, Mary Strachan became head librarian.

Bliss ignites a fire to find more firsts

In her manuscript, Lucia Bliss compiled a list of "Oswego firsts." Her list is short but inspiring: Were there more Oswego firsts? There had to be. Being historically curious and idiosyncratic, I was driven to research this.

The more I researched and read; the more I found. As of this printing, I have discovered 35 more firsts, adding to Bliss' five for a total of 40. See "Lake Oswego Firsts" (p. 182) for my complete list.

You never know where a first may lurk. Maybe you'll discover some of your own along the way.

Named for Daniel or Alphonse?

Boones Ferry Road, the Boones Ferry, Boone Bridge—many of us assumed were named for Colonel Daniel Boone. Not the case. Colonel Boone never came to Oregon. But his grandson Alphonso, Sr., came across the Oregon Trail in 1846 with his family. Alphonso and his son Jesse built the cable ferry across the Willamette River near present-day Wilsonville. It began operation in 1847.

The ferry linked fledgling Portland with the territorial government at Champoeg, and later Salem. Members of the Tuality Tribe acted as oarsmen, propelling the ferry across the river. The ferry operated 24 hours a day. Alphonso was adamant about this.

The community of Boones Landing (now Wilsonville) began around the north ferry landing. Alphonso's family cleared timber and constructed a split-log roadway leading south from the landing to Salem and north towards Portland, creating the first overland connection from Salem to the northern section of the Willamette Valley. This major thoroughfare became Boones Ferry Road. Oregon Electric Railway used a railroad bridge constructed upriver from Boone Bridge in 1907. Four miles of Boones Ferry Road go through Lake Oswego.

Alphonso Boone, Sr., was born on November 7, 1796, in Mason County, Kentucky, to Jesse Bryan Boone and Chloe Van Bibber. He moved to Missouri in the mid-1820s, eventually locating in Jefferson City where he ran a trading post from the 1830s to early 1840s, selling supplies to folks preparing to come west.

Boones Ferry Landing

Alphonso Boone married Nancy Linville, a second cousin, February 21, 1822. They had 10 children. She died in early 1839.

After his wife's death, in 1841 Boone moved to Independence, Missouri, where he continued outfitting wagon trains for the journey west. He started his own journey west in 1846 with his family and his brother-in-law, Lilburn Boggs, former Missouri governor. Boone and Boggs parted ways when Boggs heard gold calling in California. Boone continued on to the Willamette Valley, where he claimed 1,000 acres of land on the Willamette River near Charbonneau.

It wasn't long after staking his Oregon claim that Alphonso, Sr., and his sons Jesse and Alphonso, Jr., headed to California. Both sons returned home with their fortunes, but Alphonso, Sr., died February 27, 1850, of a miner's disease in the gold fields along the Feather River.

Alphonso, Jr., operated the ferry, then sold it to his brother Jesse, who operated it until his murder in 1872 at the hand of a neighbor over a river access dispute. Alphonso's daughter Chloe married Oregon Territorial Governor George Law Curry, a neighbor, in 1848.

After Jesse's untimely death, several people owned and operated the ferry before Clackamas County took it over. By the 1900s, the State of Oregon controlled it. The ferry made up to 300 trips per day, carrying up to twelve autos at a time. A reporter for a Portland newspaper wrote, "The ferry carried the public and its vehicles, from ox-drawn to diesel-driven, for over a century."

When the Baldock Freeway Bridge was built in 1954, the ferry was decommissioned and the bridge renamed Boone Bridge. Today, Boones Ferry Park in Wilsonville is located on the north shore of the Willamette at the end of one of the road fragments where the terminal was. The south shore has a marina with a boat ramp in the historical location of the other terminal. The ferry crossing site is about 2,000 feet west of the freeway and is visible from the southbound lanes of Boone Bridge. The Baldock Freeway is now known as I-5.

A Pear Tree, a Plaque, a School

Who were the Bryants? A memorial plaque at Bryant and Jean Road just west of the tennis courts reads "1853 … 1947 This stone marks the home site of Charles Wesley Bryant and his wife Mary Fay Bryant who left north Java, New York, in the spring of 1853. They traveled by covered wagon with a group of Methodist missionaries led by Rev. Harvey Hines. They arrived in October 1853 and acquired this homestead. Seven of their nine children were born and all reared in this home. Alta & Vesper, born in New York, Hale D., Ella C., Lee, Mary, Charles P., Myra, Cordelia. They were always active in church and community betterment. All honor to those courageous pioneers." The year 1947 represents the date the Citizens of Lake Oswego Committee installed the plaque.

Immediately upon arrival, Charles filed for a donation land claim—land given by the government to either a married couple (600-plus acres) or an individual (300-plus acres) at no cost. In exchange for the free land, the recipient was expected to work the land. Like others requesting donation land claims here, Charles wanted his to be along the Willamette River where the soil was fertile and would yield saleable crops. But everything had already been spoken for, so he had to settle for land that ran from what is now South Shore Boulevard along the main Oswego canal, south to the Tualatin River.

Although he didn't get the fertile land he wanted, Bryant was successful at growing hops, logging trees, and establishing prune and pear orchards. Charles Bryant built his barn and homestead where Lakeridge Middle School (formerly Waluga

Bryant farmhouse stood where Waluga Junior High used to be.

Junior High School), now stands. "Great-grandpa Charles had one of the biggest hop farms here and was one of the original hop growers," remembers Walter Durham, Jr., great-grandson of Oswego founder, Albert Alonzo Durham.

Clover was his bailiwick

Growing clover in Oregon is another Charles Bryant success story. Durham, Jr., recalls, "When Great Grandpa first arrived here, he discovered there was no red clover. He demanded to know why it wasn't grown in Oregon. Someone told him it would not grow in the Willamette Valley." Bryant's retort: "I will prove that it will grow here" [*In Their Own Words*].

Posthaste, Charles sent to New York for one bushel (eight dry gallons) of clover seed. It arrived in small packets by post the latter part of April 1854, just in time for planting on Bryant's farm. At one time, many fields of this clover—a deep, unusual shade of red—could be seen along I-205 from Oregon City to the Salem freeway. The red clover story has been well documented in the book *Seed, Soil, and Science*, written by Helen Marie Cavanaugh. Hearing of Bryant's success growing clover, Funk Seed Company agreed to sell the seed in their catalog. Sales skyrocketed from $4,500 in 1905 to $38,000 in 1908. No one ever questioned again whether red clover would grow in the Willamette Valley.

Although he cultivated his land profitably, Charles Bryant was also a skilled millwright by trade. For many years he earned a living building sawmills, from here to Spokane. Two major contributions Charles made to Oswego are the construction of Bryant Woods and the Carman House, the oldest house in Oswego. Charles Bryant built the Carman House in 1855 with his friend Waters Carman. (That name always trips me up: I want to write Carman Waters instead of Waters Carman.) The house, at the corner of Carman Drive and Wilmot Way, is one of the few remaining homes dating back to the Territorial Period, meaning before 1859. Descendants of Waters and Lucretia Carman, the first couple to marry in Oswego, have occupied the house since it was built.

Researching the Bryant family for this article led me to a typewritten letter from Mabel Bryant Meresse, dated April 26, 1964. What a find. Mabel Bryant Meresse was one of Charles and Mary Bryant's granddaughters. She wrote to Mrs. C. Gordon Livermore: "I have read your interesting article in the *Genealogical Forum Bulletin* about the cemetery on the Bryant Place. At one time there were four graves at the lower part of the old orchard. In 1889 these gravestones were moved to River View (Cemetery). Three were children of my grandparents

Mary Fay and Charles Bryant—Lee, Vesper, and Mary. The other little grave was their granddaughter Nellie Anderson, five years old, daughter of Alta Bryant and Asbury Anderson."

My historical curiosity makes me wonder if the placement of the Bryant plaque is in the vicinity of where the four gravestones were. As you look at the plaque, you can't help notice the lone 40-foot pear tree growing nearby, probably left as a memorial to the family pear orchard. Fire destroyed the Bryant family homestead (no date).

Charles Wesley Bryant and Mary Elvira Fay were married January 31, 1849 three years before coming to Oregon. They celebrated a 60th wedding anniversary in 1909 at the home of their daughter, E.L. Lane. Mary passed away shortly afterward, at 80. Charles died October 26, 1915, at 88. Both are buried at River View Cemetery. According to Walter Durham, Jr., in *Lake Oswego Review* article, "all of the Bryant children made significant contributions to education in Lake Oswego and down the Willamette Valley."

Bryant Elementary School…Bryant Station…Bryant Woods…Bryant Road…Bryant Nature Park. Thank you, Charles Wesley Bryant, another of Oswego's influential early pioneers.

Saying goodbye to Bryant Elementary

The demolition of Bryant Elementary School fueled a lot of fond memories from previous students. Here are a some posted on *Lake Oswego Review's* Facebook page: Brent DeBoer: "Bryant beavers is our name. Being awesome is our game. We all wear blue and gold. Our school spirit is bright and bold!!" Hayley C. Platt: "My grandma taught at Bryant!" Kristin

Z. Kohorst: "I went to Bryant for grades 1–6, late 1970s–early 1980s. My teachers were: Mrs. Ross, Ms. Ikeberg, Mrs. Honzel, Mrs. Oliver, Mr. Williams, Mr. Young. Mrs. Fairbaren was the principal, Mrs. Sharp was the librarian, Mr. Latham was my music teacher and Mr. Dominic Yambsu was my PE teacher." Brittany Zika: "One of my tiles is up there!!!"

Mosaic wall art project at Bryant Elementary School
AUTHOR'S COLLECTION

Along with distinctive mosaic tile artwork, another of Bryant Elementary's unique characteristics was the hexagonal-shaped classroom clusters referred to as pods. There were three pods consisting of six classrooms each for a total of 18 rooms. Centered in each cluster was a room for storage and group instruction. Moveable walls, which allowed teachers to combine classes if needed without a lot of disruption, were also unique to the school.

Between the clusters was a covered play area, and a multi-purpose building with stage, offices, carpeted library, conference room, and resource room where tapes, filmstrips, and records were available to students. Connecting the clusters to the main building were two corridors that ran along each side. Outside walkways connected the clusters.

Bryant Elementary had two kindergarten classrooms. Although they were not part of the clusters, the classrooms were six-sided. Storage facilities and bathrooms were in a corridor between the two rooms. Architects for the school were Hewlett (Palmer A.) and Jamison (James W.), who also designed the Sisters of St. Mary's campus. General Contractor was Contractor's, Inc. Construction of the new school began November 1, 1965, and was ready for students the following September, 1966. Enrollment that first year was 460.

Test your Bryant Elementary School IQ . . .

a. When was Bryant Elementary built?
b. Who was Bryant's principal when it opened?
c. School superintendent?
d. How many square feet is Bryant Elementary?
e. Total number of classrooms?
f. Mascot?
g. School colors?
h. What were Bryant's two unique design features?
i. Cost to build the school?
j. Who is the school named after?
k. Did the school have a cafeteria?
l. What does Waluga mean?

ANSWERS: a. 1966; b. Charles Actor; c. Dr. Russell Esvelt; d. 47,260; e. 20; f. Beaver; g. gold & blue; h. classroom clusters and covered play area; i. $608,146; j. Charles Wesley Bryant; k. no cafeteria, but had a kitchen; l. Black Swan

Surgeon, Physician, Musician

"**I DON'T REALLY KNOW** why I went into medicine," William Cane told the *Lake Oswego Review* in a 1980 interview. "Both my Dad and my grandfather were MDs, so maybe that explains it. What it doesn't explain is why I became a surgeon before becoming an internist. Most medical students become internists, then go on to become surgeons."

Dr. Cane received his medical degree from Washington University in St. Louis in 1928. That same year he married Winifred, his high school sweetheart. Cane interned at Henry Ford Hospital in Detroit and came to Oregon in 1930 where he had been appointed an instructor in surgical procedures at the University of Oregon Medical School. In 1946, he was appointed a fellow in the prestigious American College of Surgeons. Apparently, it was serendipitous that he became a surgeon before becoming an internist.

Dr. William H. Cane at 77
LAKE OSWEGO REVIEW

During the Depression, Dr. Cane went to work for the Portland Police Bureau to make ends meet, as the police surgeon. The job involved everything: taking care of derelicts, drug addicts,

Second Stop: Nancy Writes (articles A–L) • 33

injuries off the street, even helping a little girl whose Easter bunny bit off the end of her finger, bone and all.

Cane traveled through North Africa as part of a medical team during WWII. When the war ended, he returned to Oregon, opening his own practice in Oswego where the Goodyear Tire Store was on 3rd Street.

Dr. Cane practiced there until he purchased the Murphy building from the Ladd Estate Company in 1939. He remodeled Paul C. Murphy's office building to accommodate his medical practice and residence.

When he came to Oswego in 1932, Cane recalled there was only one other doctor in town and the population was about 1,500. By 1980, the population had increased to 21,000 and the city had several doctors. The good doctor was a member of the original Community Club, which became the Oswego Chamber of Commerce.

George Kent, a close friend, recalled that Cane was also a musician. He played the violin and also collected them, which accounts for the fact that he had many hanging on his walls and used them to decorate his shutters. In the museum room of the Oswego Heritage House and Museum, a pair of shutters has several small "f"-looking cutouts on them. Those "f's" represent the "f" strut on the violin. The shutters originally served as cabinet doors in Cane's kitchen. Dr. Cane also collected music stands and *New Yorker* cartoons. When he wasn't playing the violin or practicing medicine, he was working on his golf game. He was an avid golfer who played many courses around the world.

Other friends—and patients—recall that Dr. Cane kept his "drugs" in wastebaskets. He figured if someone broke in, they would never think to look in a wastebasket for them. The City of Lake Oswego had to get after the good doctor because he was dumping the chemicals used to develop his x-rays down the drains that ran into the sewer system.

It is rumored that Cane did not trust banks and had a vault built underneath his house when he remodeled it. When the Oswego Heritage Council renovated the house, several gold coins worth about $10,000 were found stashed away in in the walls.

Dr. Cane retired in the 1970s—when—according to Kent—his medical malpractice insurance got too expensive. He remained in the house until 1996, when his wife passed away. At that time, Cane moved into a nursing home in Portland, leaving the property and the home vacant and unattended.

Memories of Dr. Cane

Trista Nelson, a patient, recalled Cane piercing her ears. The piercings weren't level and the earrings didn't hang evenly. When Nelson told him, he just re-pierced one of the holes at an angle instead of piercing 2 new holes at the same level.

Carolyn Mays wrote the following to the Oswego Heritage Council in response to the History Connection article I wrote about Dr. Cane:

"I attended Dr. Cane's estate sale at the home and vividly remember two things. The family room was wonderful—kind of rustic with a rock fireplace and rustic timber mantle and beams on the ceiling. The cool thing though, was that across the mantle and on each beam was a Bible verse or famous quote hand-scripted in chalk. The handwriting was as beautiful as the verses.

"The other unique memory was the dining room. There were plantation-type shutters on the windows with signatures/autographs penned on each slat, depicting many of the celebrities and dignitaries Dr. Cane and his wife are rumored to have entertained in the home. Being in the home definitely gave me a sense of what an eclectic, unique individual[s] Dr. Cane and his wife must have been."

Dr. William Cane passed away September 23, 1998.

Shipley-Cook Farmstead

TWO EARLY SETTLERS who made significant contributions to Oswego history were Adam Randolph Shipley and James Preston Cook. Both men came from Ohio across the Oregon Trail to settle in Oswego. Shipley came in 1852; Cook came thirty years later in 1883.

Adam Shipley—better known as A.R. Shipley—married Celinda Himes in 1854. They had four sons and two daughters: Milton, Lester, Alphonso Wood, Randolph Chaplain, Macinda (Cindy) and Cora.

A.R. established a farmstead in what settlers called Hazelia—the area south of McVey extending to the Tualatin River, along its banks for some distance and along Stafford Road. Hazelia derived its name from the hazel brush which grew in abundance here. Hazel brush is a small, shrubby tree found in woodlands, gardens and grasslands. Well known for its long male catkins (known as lambs' tails) which appear green in spring, the catkins then ripen to brown followed by the yellow fruits—known to us as "hazelnuts"—in late summer. Prolific in growth as it might be, it takes fifteen years for hazel brush to produce fruit.

The original Shipley farmstead, which still stands today, consisted of a barn (built before the farmhouse), a chicken coop, the farmhouse, woodshed, and eventually a grange hall and Hazelia schools. Built in the 1860s just south of the Rosemont roundabout, the farmhouse had ten rooms with bath, two fireplaces, and an ever-so-important pantry.

The woodshed was built with rooms above it to house the hired help, many of whom were Chinese. Chung, a favorite servant, preferred living in a small place of his own by the creek behind the farmhouse instead of sharing living quarters. Evidence that Chinese workers occupied the rooms above the woodshed is a newspaper from 1890 plastered on the wall.

Fondly called "Father Shipley," A.R. was one of the first to import and grow grapes in Oregon. He imported several varieties from Europe; other varieties he ordered from his home in Ohio. When asked what three varieties one should plant for selling, he replied "I plant three hundred Concords first, second I plant three hundred Concords, and third, I plant three hundred more Concords."

Adam Randolph Shipley inspired the formation of Oswego Grange No. 175, which provided a place for social events and served as a schoolhouse for local children. The first grange hall was built on a large hill on his land halfway up the butte (now Cooks Butte). On the top of the hill was the burial ground of the Willamette Native Americans. Shipley protected the sacred burial ground, never allowing anyone to go near it. A small trail leading up the hill was the only way to reach the building. The Oswego Grange occupied the building until 1890.

Shipley served as the first Oswego Grange Master and was elected State Grange Master twice, serving from 1875 to 1880. He also served as second postmaster of Portland for several years, and led Sunday School classes at Oswego's First Methodist Church. In addition, he was a charter member of the Odd Fellows Lodge. In 1891, Adam Shipley was appointed to the Board of Regents at the State Agricultural College (now Oregon State University) and also served as librarian for a time.

J.P. Cook arrives in Oswego in 1883

James Preston Cook came to Oregon after hearing about the need for iron workers in Oswego. He worked at the foundry for a while and also worked on the Shipley farm. Cook held various other jobs, finally earning enough money to purchase the farm in 1900 from Shipley. One of his jobs was working construction on the railroad between Portland and Dundee. (Cook Station is named after him.) Cook was also active in the grange started by Adam Shipley. The butte west of the farm complex, where Cook raised livestock, was coined Cooks Butte. The Cook farm was often a gathering place for the community, and James and his wife Susie started a 4th of July gathering with homemade ice cream that is still celebrated by the Cook family today.

James P. and Susie B. Cook with son William
PHOTO COURTESY
COOK FAMILY COLLECTION

J.P. died in 1931; his wife Susie in 1947. Son William took over the farm. Like Shipley, he was active in the grange, Odd Fellows, and the school district. He was also a local historian, and a charter member of the Oswego Fire Department. The family cultivated fruit trees; grew a variety of crops; raised livestock and sold cream to the dairy in Lake Oswego. William's wife Sara Ethel loved to quilt. (Read the story about the Cook quilts on page 39.) William Sr. died In 1960; Sarah Ethel died in 1967. After their deaths sons, William Jr. and James inherited the farm, each owning a half interest. William sold his part of the acreage to James, who deeded the farm to his son Rick in the mid 1990s.

Rick Cook currently lives on and manages the Shipley-Cook Farmstead. Eugene Wine Cellar leases a portion of the acreage to grow Marchael Foch grapes for wine-making. Many of the activities that happened at the farm during the 1850s still occur today. Every Christmas, several members of the Cook family make candy from recipes handed down through five

Shipley-Cook Farmstead showing barn and farmhouse
COOK FAMILY COLLECTION

generations. Rick's brother Steve tends the chicken coop and is the fudgemeister; Rick is the brittlemeister; several nieces and nephews tend plots of vegetables. Keeping with the tradition of family gatherings, every 4th of July the Cook Clan holds a large family picnic at the farmstead, with attendees numbering around a hundred, including friends and neighbors.

A few words about the barn: It is a rare example of an Oregon Pioneer–era agricultural building, as a study conducted by the State Historic Preservation Office found that 95 percent of the Willamette Valley's pioneer properties (1841–1865) have been destroyed. The Shipley-Cook barn was constructed with hand-hewn timbers using mortise-and-tenon joints. If you were to peek inside, you would see several *very* large saw blades—the kind used for felling timber—hanging on the wall, plus a great many other relics and artifacts.

Certificates of merit awarded to the Shipley-Cook Farmstead

- Placed on County Historic Resource list 1989
- Clackamas County Historic Landmark 1992
- Vineyard established 1992
- Received Century Farm designation 2000
- Placed on National Register of Historic Places 2008
- Received Oregon and Clackamas County Heritage Tree designation 2012
- Oswego Heritage Council Historic Home Tour 2017
- Dedication of Hazelia Agri-Cultural Heritage Trail 2017
- Cooks Butte named after the Cook Family

Cook Connection to Quilts Dates Back 100 Years

"**MY GREAT GRANDMOTHER** and my grandmother stitched a quilt they called "Hearts and Gizzards,"" relates Rick Cook proudly. "They say this quilt won ribbons at state and county fairs. I would like to display the Hearts and Gizzards pattern on the west side of our barn at the Shipley-Cook Farmstead overlooking the chicken coop." Displaying a quilt pattern painted on a piece of plywood and mounted on the side of a barn was inspired by the Quilt Barn Trail Project of Washington County (see https://tualatinvalley.org/local-favorites/tours-routes-trails/quilt-barn-trail/).

Hearts and Gizzards
COOK FAMILY COLLECTION

"Grandma also made the Crazy Quilt," Cook comments. "She named it that because of all the different stitches friends taught her when they would bring pieces of velvet and other fabrics for her to use. The maroon velvet border came from my great grandmother's wedding dress. Grandma started the quilt when she was 11, after having polio, then set it aside for several years, finishing it in 1959 as a gift for my Dad's 30th birthday."

Inspired to preserve the legacy of the Cook family quilts, plus contribute to the Quilt Index Project, Rick Cook took ten family heirloom quilts—some quilted 100 years ago—to Lake Oswego

Montavilla Sewing Center in September of 2017 to be examined and documented. A project of Michigan State University, the Quilt Index is a national digital clearinghouse of thousands of stories, images, and information about quilts, quiltmakers and the quilting process drawn from hundreds of private and public collections around the world (see https://quiltindex.org).

The Oregon Quilt Project had a run of ten years, launched in 2009 and completed in 2019. It was a group of dedicated volunteers who collected, documented, and input information about quilts and quilt makers in Oregon for the national Quilt Index database. The project operated under the auspices of the Willamette Heritage Center in Salem, located at the historic Thomas Kay Woolen Mill.

"It was a very interesting day," recalls Cook about the two-part documentation process. "I received in the mail a quilt history form for each quilt, which I had to complete and bring to my documentation appointment, then there is a physical inspection of the quilt. Trained volunteers from the Oregon Quilt Project review the history and the forms, and conduct the physical inspection."

During the look-see part of the documentation, the quilt is opened flat on a table resembling a bed frame. Information about the batting, top, back, and condition are recorded. Then it is measured and its pattern noted, using several universally accepted references. Next, a photograph of the quilt(s) is taken and the owner receives a registration number for each quilt submitted, which is to be sewn on the back of the quilt. If the owner decides to share the information and photo on the Quilt Index, a release form is signed.

Cook notes that all ten documented quilts are now in the Quilt Index database. "Since its inception 10 years ago, The Oregon Quilt Project has documented 1,500 quilts," noted Mary Bywaters Cross, quilt historian, author, and Oregon Quilt Project board member in 2017, "and we hope to have documented hundreds more by the time the project ends in the spring of 2018."

Mary Bywaters Cross and Joan Beck, Oregon Quilt Project volunteers, shared this story about the reunion of the Gere family quilts. One quilt had been officially documented by Oregon Quilt Project volunteers at a documentation day in eastern Oregon. Identified as a Redwork pattern—red embroidery on a white background—the pattern is a series of circles depicting names of the Gere family. Every year, the quilt, referred to as the wedding quilt, is handed down to the oldest member of the family. As far as they knew, the quilt had never left the family.

Imagine the surprise when a quilt of the same Redwork pattern of names embroidered in circles of red thread was brought to a different documentation day in a different location. Oregon Quilt Project volunteers knew they had seen the pattern before. Is it possible there was a second quilt that the Gere family never knew about? They invited the Geres to come (from eastern Oregon) to documentation day in Lake Oswego, and they invited the owner of the second one, a Lake Oswego woman who received the quilt from a friend, to bring her quilt.

Placing the quilts side by side, volunteers confirmed both quilts had been made by the Gere family. The Lake Oswego owner graciously offered to sell her quilt back to the Geres.

Although the Geres now possess the two quilts, how the quilts became separated remains a mystery.

The word quilt comes from the Latin *culcita,* meaning a stuffed sack, but it came into the English language from the French word *cuilte*. The origins of quilting remain unknown, but historians have recorded that quilting, piecing, and applique were used for clothing and furnishings in diverse parts of the world in early times.

Savior of the Sequoia

"I HOPE THAT WHEN I am gone from here others will carry on in the same way even if they forget my name," Mary Holmes Goodall said in an oral history interview with Theresa Truchot in 1973.

Not only was Goodall a stalwart preservationist, she was also a historian, a journalist, and a civic leader. Goodall's book, *Oregon's Iron Dream,* written in 1958, was inspired by Lucia Bliss' 1944 manuscript, "The Foundation: Early History of Oswego, Oregon." While attending Oregon State, Goodall worked as a college correspondent, covering football games. As she put it, "I loved this job because I got to meet all the football players." When Mary graduated, her first official newspaper job as a journalist began at *The Oregonian*.

Goodall left *The Oregonian* after giving birth to her two sons. However, money was tight. Goodall wanted to go back to work, hoping she would be able to work at home. A job at *The Oregon Journal* offered her that opportunity, and that is where she launched the well-known "Mary Cullen's Kitchen," a column devoted to cooking and fashion.

The name Mary Cullen derived from Goodall's first name Mary and cullen from the word culinary. Goodall states in her interview with Truchot she could never use the name for her own because the *Journal* patented it. Mary Cullen's Kitchen became so well-read that soon Goodall also had her own radio show. Goodall stated in Truchot's book, "I did my biggest cooking and fashion shows at the Civic Auditorium. It was a great experience."

Goodall left *The Oregon Journal* when her husband Ken's business, Goodall Oil Company, began to flourish to the point where she didn't have to work. Although she left *The Oregon Journal* behind, she didn't leave writing behind. She explains:

"When Ken went to the legislature, I accompanied him as his secretary. I wrote magazine material and feature stories for *Sunset* magazine and various Sunday newspapers on the coast. At the same time I was also writing political columns for three different newspapers.

"And, I also authored two European travelogues. As I was writing one of the travelogues, I realized I must come home and write the history of my dear little town before it lost all traces of the iron era which gave it such character.

"I turned out *Oregon's Iron Dream* with twenty-five friends who helped with the research and I donated my royalties to the Friends of the Library for a new library building. We now do own a halfa block."

In addition to being a published author and writer, Mary Goodall served on the Lake Oswego City Council for eight years. She worked tirelessly for the beautification and preservation of great old trees. During her tenure on the City Council, an ordinance passed on tree cutting, which had been unrestricted prior to this.

Goodall single-handedly spearheaded the effort to save the giant Sequoia tree located in the corner of the Safeway property at 4th Street and A Avenue. A City Council member in 1964, Goodall approached Safeway store officials bringing to their attention the beauty of the *Big Sequoia* and what a shame it would be to cut it down. Store officials agreed not to sacrifice the tree for three parking spaces. As a result of Goodall's preservation triumph, the sequoia became "our town Christmas tree." The lighting of *Big Sequoia* the day after Thanksgiving has become a Lake Oswego tradition and is now an annual community-wide event kickstarting the beginning of the holiday season.

When the tree was first lit in 1964 or 1965, 2,200 lights adorned the *giant* 80-foot tree. The lights were provided by Safeway but strung by the City. However, as the tree grew, it became more difficult to string lights, so the tree is now lit with large snowflakes.

A little about Mary Goodall's family

Mary's grandparents, Richard and Marian Knight, came from England and met in Colorado. Educated in Belgium at a Quaker school, her grandfather became an apothecary. They moved to Portland in 1883 and lived in the Pittock block, next to their friends the Pittocks. Richard opened a drugstore here, close to the old Multnomah Stadium.

Later they moved to 18th and Chapman, the site of the Zion Lutheran Church designed by the renown architect Pietro Belluschi. Grandfather Knight used to work the late shift at the drugstore and would walk home past Multnomah Stadium, previously a Chinese vegetable garden.

Many sailing ships from the United Kingdom came to Portland for wheat in those days. The captains use to call at the Knight Drug Company to find out what was happening in town, often bringing monkeys, parakeets, and other animals to him for safe keeping. Finally, Knight started a roadside zoo at 3rd and Morrison Street. Ladies stopped their carriages to view the animals and to buy drug supplies.

Grandmother Knight subtlety suggested that perhaps Portland needed a zoo. Husband Richard agreed wholeheartedly. He approached Portland City Council with the idea and offered his stock to them. Of course, there was no money in the budget for such a venture, but if Dr. Knight and his family would go out every day and feed them and clean the cages, the City would take the animals and house them in cages taken from a defunct traveling circus. Thus, Mary Holmes Goodall's grandfather and grandmother founded the Portland Zoo.

Mary's mother, Edith Knight, wrote for *The Oregonian* under the pen name Marian Miller. Mary's sister Florence also studied at Oregon State. She won a scholarship to Harvard School of Landscape where she studied landscape architecture. Upon returning to Portland, Florence took a job with the City of Portland planning several parks as their landscape architect. Her claim to fame: design of the International Rose Test Garden at Washington Park and the landscaping at Lloyd Center.

Mary Goodall was born in 1899 in southern California; she passed away in 1989 at 90.

Her legacy lives on

Mary Goodall *loved* Lake Oswego; she served our city well as a harbinger of preservation and a great steward for promoting historic legacy. Among her many accomplishments, she...

- authored the book, *Oregon's Iron Dream*
- wrote Mary Cullen's Kitchen column for *The Oregon Journal*
- saved the historic "Peg Tree"
- helped found the Festival of the Arts
- served on Lake Oswego City Council for eight years
- saved the giant Sequoia at 5th & A—now the city's holiday tree
- served as honorary trustee of the Lake Oswego Junior Historical Society

An Island in Oswego Lake?

During the Great Depression, Oswego Lake provided the perfect setting—fishing, swimming, canoeing, and boating—for real estate developers and merchants to promote their products.

Jantzen Knitting Mills promoted its swimsuits bearing the provocative logo "Red Diving Girl," using Oswego Lake as the backdrop. The diving girl in the ad was inspired by Lake Oswego resident and developer Ann Schukart, who was seen diving off Jantzen Bridge into the lake. The "Red Diving Girl" logo first appeared in Jantzen catalogs in 1920. The Sons of Neptune, a Portland aquatic club, wore Jantzen swimsuits in a canoe pageant on the lake in 1938.

Halvorson Island bridge designed by architect Richard Sundeleaf

Carl Jantzen, owner and founder of Jantzen Knitting Mills, purchased the four-acre Crazy Man's Island from the Ladd Estate Company in 1929 for $50,000. He later renamed it Jantzen Island.

According to local lore, settlers called the property Crazy Man's Island because an eccentric recluse lived there for several years who acted crazy, screaming and yelling if people tried to talk to him. He was often seen in town picking up mail or shopping.

Jantzen hired the firm of Ertz and Burns to design the house. He first asked Richard Sundeleaf, who designed the Jantzen Knitting Mills factories, to design the plans; but his wife Emma threw a fit, saying emphatically, "No factory architect is going to design my house!"

Sundeleaf was relegated to designing the bridge and boathouse. He worked with Tommy Thompson, noted California designer of the Santa Anna racetrack gardens, to create the landscaping for the mansion gardens. The terraces, benches, and arbors were the perfect setting for many outdoor recreational activities. Jantzen used the mansion to host swimming parties where he displayed the latest in swimming attire to his guests.

Known as "Carneita," named after the Jantzen children Carl and Oneita, the Jantzen estate reflected a medieval theme that matched the island's setting. The bridge and water lapping the island's edges conjured up visions of castle drawbridges and moats. Architects used stone, a tower, and turrets to create the medieval motif.

Current owners, Rick and Erica Miller, purchased the island in 2012. Rick Miller is the chairman of Avamere Group.

Previous owners include: Jerry Stubblefield, founder of Avia footwear (1987); Carl Halvorson, developer of Mountain Park (1956); and Harry Coffee, an insurance agent (1952). Carl Halvorson and his family were the longest-staying owners, having lived on the island for three decades, which is why the property is now known as Halvorson Island.

1947 Lake Grove School

Flames Could Be Seen from Afar

A SIX-ALARM FIRE BROKE OUT at 9:50 P.M. on February 10, 1948. Diane Gilbert lived so close to Lake Grove School, she remembered seeing the flames from her front yard. School board member Edith Zimmerman recollected: "We had all worked hard getting a piano for the school, a real luxury. I remember the next day seeing the burned mass in the basement." Tualatin Valley Builders Supply, located just across the street from the entrance of the school, had its north-facing windows blown out, according to one of the employees. The school's main entrance was right on Boones Ferry Road.

Although the school and all its equipment and supplies were destroyed, the buses, housed in a separate building, were not affected by the massive blaze. As luck would have it, another, larger school building was under construction on the same site at the time of the fire. The new building did not sustain any damage, because it was sited far enough away from the original in what was then a wheat field. Cause of the blaze: explosion of a water heater, according to the fire department.

Prior to Lake Grove School, three schools were built in the area: Springbrook 1, Springbrook 2, Springbrook 3—all named for the creek that flows into the north side of the lake. Mary Goodall (*Oregon's Iron Dream*) writes that the first Springbrook School, built in 1861, was located next to the creek at the intersection of Wembley Park Road and Twin Fir Road, on land donated by Etta Carman, one of Waters Carman's three daughters, who received a third of her father's property when he died. Goodall goes on to say that Agnes Nelson was one of the school's most beloved teachers.

Springbrook 2, according to Goodall, was built in 1904 by Wilbur Wilmot's neighbors, on land he donated that was near his peach orchard at the intersection of Upper Boones Ferry Road (now Upper Drive) and Lower Boones Ferry Road. Springbrook 3, continues Goodall, was located in Alto Park, the area north of Mountain Park where Stephenson Road is.

John Stone (*In Their Own Words* oral history interview) remembered, "I attended Springbrook 1 in 1902. The school was one room. Other pupils who went there were the Worthingtons (Bill, Howard, Mary, Nina, Orlando), The Meyers (Bill and Robert), The Kruses (Jessie and Frances), The Platts (Ben and Rocky), The McCurrys (Grace and Leola), and a Bill Cook from the Hazelia area." Stone goes on to say that he attended that school for only two years because he had moved on to the high school level.

Herbert Lechter Nelson (*In Their Own Words*) claimed there was a Fernwood school built in Lake Grove. I couldn't confirm this, but Gretchen Barber remembers going to first grade there with her friend, Mary Nelson. Gretchen's dad, Ward C. Smith, remembered that Miss Stone taught in a one-room schoolhouse called Fernwood. Could they have meant Springbrook?

Will Pomeroy, son of Superintendent of Mines for Oregon Iron and Steel, James Pomeroy, wrote in his diary (*The Diary of Will Pomeroy*, edited by Claire Kellogg and Susana Kuo) on April 16, 1883 that "school is commenced at Spring Brook today." Pomeroy went to Springbrook from April through August.

The town of Lake Grove was platted in 1912. The name came from all the groves of fir trees—as far as the eye could see—in the area, and the town's close proximity to the lake. As the town began to grow, so did the need for more than just one- and two-room schoolhouses. Lake Grove School was built in 1924 on the southwest corner of the present site, where the playground is. Built with a wood frame support structure, the school was single-story. It had a half-underground concrete basement and an auditorium, but no gym.

The gym and additional classrooms on the north side of the building were added on after 1948. A new covered playground was installed in 1990; in 1992 landscaping and a beautiful brick courtyard and art sculpture were added—a nice welcoming touch.

Although the 1924 structure was a total loss, students were back in class in the new building only 13 days after the fire—February 23, 1948—but only those in the primary grades, and they had to go in two shifts. Plans for the new school called for a total of eighteen classrooms, but since only eight could be completed quickly, students in 7th and 8th grades attended school in nearby churches.

After graduation from eighth grade, students went to either West Linn High or Lincoln High. There was no Oswego High. No one in the community was convinced there were enough people living here to support it, even though it would have been built on donated land in a central location. Lake Oswego High School was built in 1951. In 1953 Lake Grove School became part of the Lake Oswego School District. Prior to that, it was its own district.

Original Lake Grove Fire Station

Fanning the Flames of History

I HAVE LIVED IN Lake Grove for 25 years; driven past the fire station at Bryant and Sunset Roads thousands of times, and always wondered about that building; but never bothered to find out... until now. What a surprise... the building was designed by well-known architect Richard Sundeleaf! I know the name Sundeleaf because he was the featured architect of the Oswego Heritage Council's Historic Home Tour in 2012. I was aware that he'd designed several homes and commercial buildings in Lake Oswego, but I never knew about this treasure. His architectural designs reflect the characteristics associated with Minimal Traditional buildings: one- to one-and-a-half stories, minimal to no overhangs, moderately pitched roofs, board-and-batten horizontal siding, simple modern trim and details.

Designed in 1947 and constructed in 1955, the building was abandonded as a firehouse in 1990 when a new fire department facility was constructed at Bryant and Jean Roads. The original firehouse has retained its historic Sundeleaf integrity through the years, and today serves as a community meeting place.

Lake Oswego's first fire department was organized in 1910 and consisted of five volunteers. "Red McVey was the heartbeat of the fire department," according to Don Farmer, a friend of McVey's and a former volunteer. The other four serving with McVey were Chief George Miller, Edgar Davidson, George Prosser, and William Cook. The volunteer firefighters, often referred to as "smoke eaters," received $1.00 for each weekly drill they attended, plus $1.00 for each fire.

Firefighting equipment during those early years was no more than a bucket brigade consisting of twelve leather buckets mounted on posts and buildings around the city, two 24-foot wooden ladders, two axes that hung on poles at 2nd Street and and A Avenue, and a two-wheeled, hand-pulled hose cart.

The first piece of moving equipment was a Studebaker sedan confiscated during prohibition and unclaimed, which the volunteer firefighters purchased from the city for $1. They converted it into a truck for $555. It took two people to get the thing going, because it had to be hand cranked. The first to arrive would start it—one would stand on the throttle and the other would crank.

Another piece of firefighting equipment was the purchase of a school bell in 1915. It was mounted on a steel water tower (not sure of the location of the bell) donated by John F. Bickner, a member of Oswego's first City Council. Today, the bell is mounted in front of the fire station on B Avenue.

In 1925, the City purchased "Old Jimmy," a 1923 GMC K-16, from Wentworth and Irwin. (Dot connection: My Dad used to lease vehicles for his business from Wentworth and Irwin.) Before taking delivery of the K-16, Wentworth and Irwin transformed the truck into a working fire engine. They installed a 500-gallons-per-minute centrifuge water pump powered by a 25-horsepower engine. The truck had an open cab—with all this rain?—for getting in and out quickly. K-16 was retired in 1957. It sat in a warehouse for several years where it was completely submerged in the flood of 1964. But it survived. After several fire department members got hit by a wave of nostalgia, it was decided that K-16 should be restored. Relying mostly on their own skills and finances, restoration efforts began in the early 1970s. Now "Old Jimmy" sits proudly in the lobby of the main fire station, looking as shiny and glamorous as ever.

The next piece of equipment acquired after the confiscated Studebaker was an ambulance. McVey felt this was a necessity after G.E. Cheney (grandfather of my friend Jan Newton Becker) suffered a heart attack at Al Hughes' service station and had to wait hours for an ambulance. A Ford panel truck was purchased. This was later traded for a used Cadillac ambulance. That was traded for a $10,000 Cadillac ambulance in 1957. Since there is a lake in our midst, the Lake Oswego Fire Departmemt has a unique piece of fire-fighting equipment—a fire-fighting boat—which was launched in 1937.

Murder in Lake Oswego?

DECEMBER 16, 1941, Lake Oswego Hunt Club was the site of a murder. Occupying 20 acres on Iron Mountain Road where it meets Lakeview Blvd., Lake Oswego Hunt is a 75-year-old horseback-riding facility that is listed on the National Historic Register due to its original wooden trusses, which are still in tact.

The grooms' quarters is where the murder took place, at about 3:00 A.M. It involved two stable hands, Clarence McPherson —who also used the name John Buhl—and David Smith, according to local research historian Steve Dietz. Smith and McPherson were playing blackjack when they got into an argument. Smith accused McPherson of cheating, because he was winning all the money. He tried to take the winnings back, but McPherson refused to hand it over. The story goes that Smith then hit McPherson with a water bucket. McPherson retaliated by shooting Smith in the lower abdomen with a .22 caliber rifle.

Observing all of this was John Henderson, another stable hand. Henderson, along with several other workers, left the bunkhouse shortly after the mishap to do their jobs. None of them bothered to notify the manager that an employee had been shot. Smith died seven hours after he was shot. His body was discovered by C.J. Hollingsworth, manager of The Hunt, who called officials.

McPherson was arrested by Clackamas County Sheriff Fred Reaksecker and placed in the county jail. He was arraigned in

Oswego justice court. The DA wanted a first-degree murder charge, but the jury convicted McPherson of second-degree murder, which carries a mandatory life sentence. McPherson served seven years in the Oregon State Penitentiary and was then paroled. His whereabouts after parole are a little unclear, but based on Dietz's research, we

Murder occurred in one of the bunk rooms above the barn where the windows are.

PHOTO COURTESY LAKE OSWEGO HUNT CLUB

can assume that he probably returned to Arizona—his home state—where he remained until his death. An obituary stating that McPherson was a WWI veteran and a death certificate showing that a Clarence McPherson died in Veterans Hospital in Phoenix leads us to conclude that this was the same man. McPherson also served in the 10th Cavalry Regiment of Buffalo Soldiers. "Buffalo Soldiers" was a term used by the U.S. Army that referred to units comprised of African Americans whose service earned them an honored place in U.S. history.

A Grand Dame Was She in 1893

Oswego Public School (built 1893, demolished 1928), became Lakewood School

OSWEGO PUBLIC SCHOOL, built as a three-story structure in 1893, reflected the Victorian-style architecture of the times. The school employed a principal and three teachers; Mary Bickner was one of the teachers. The town's tallest building at the time, Oswego's Grand Dame came down 35 years later to make way for Lakewood School.

Arsenius DeBauw remembered the original school was "up on the hill, where the Lakewood School is, right on that spot" (Theresa Truchot, *In Their Own Words*).

Originally called Oswego Grammar School, Lakewood School was built in 1928 in the Colonial Revival–style architecture we see today. When Lakewood School was built, Oswego's population was barely 1200. By 1978 it had soared to 20,000. When the school could no longer support the educational needs of the community, it was closed. In 1979, Lakewood Theater Company, now Lakewood Center for the Arts, purchased the building from the school district to be used as a performing arts center. Lakewood School is the oldest public building in continual use today.

The architect, Luther Lee Dougan, was a prominent Portland architect who moved here in 1903 from Princeton, Indiana, after attending Armour Institute of Technology in Chicago and Kansas State University. One of his first jobs was as an office boy for architect Frank Lloyd Wright. He also worked for the well-known architectural firm of A.E. Doyle and for Aaron Gould before partnering with Chester Houghtalling to form Houghtalling and Dougan in 1915. The firm designed Portland's Washington High School in 1922 in the Classic Revival architectural style but on a larger and grander scale than the Lakewood School building.

Cost to build Lakewood ... $65,000.

Inspired by Greek and Roman design, Classic Revival architecture is represented by massive columns with decorated capitals. Capitals are the broad section of a column usually at the top. Classic Revival architecture is said to represent strength and was frequently used for public buildings such as schools, banks, libraries, museums, government buildings.

Oswego education begins in 1856

Oswego first began educating its youngsters in 1856. Students commuted across the Willamette River by canoe or barge to a log cabin at Risley Landing. Oswego had no official space designated for learning in those early days, so "schooling" was a joint effort between the communities of Gladstone, Oak Grove and Jennings Lodge. Only 15 students attended that first year and the school session was only six weeks; the budget was $72.

According to a manuscript written by Lucia Bliss, Oswego's first librarian—also historian and teacher—there was a building constructed on Furnace Street in "Old Town" Oswego that served as a schoolhouse. Bliss states that George Durham was the teacher. The Lake Oswego Library has a copy of her manuscript titled "The Foundation: Early History of Oswego, Oregon."

Schooling takes place in many venues

In 1868 or '69, school was conducted in the front room of the newly built Locey home. Mrs. Ann Locey was one of the teachers. Also in 1868, the city of Oswego decided to form its own school district, and Oswego School District No. 47 was organized February 10, 1868. Oswego had its own district but no classroom: "Old Dooley's" vacant saloon on Ladd Street became a classroom. The bar was pushed out of the way and a few rough benches brought in. Lizzie Libby taught in the makeshift saloon schoolroom in 1879. The school session by now had increased from six weeks to three months.

According to Lucia Bliss, financial support for the three-month-long school sessions was based on a subscription that each family promised to pay. Teachers boarded at pupils' homes. After the makeshift schoolroom in the saloon, the grange hall became the next classroom in 1891. There were three teachers at the time: H.T. Evans, principal—$57.50/month; Miss H.M. Wetherell (intermediate)—$40/month; and Miss Mary Bickner (primary)—$40/month. The school had yet another new location on the corner of Durham and Wilbur Streets. Miss Bliss arrived in Lake Oswego from Germany with her parents in the spring of 1892. She attended school at the Grange Hall. Her teacher was Mr. Evans, the principal, who also taught the older children.

The Grange Hall was replaced in 1893 by a more formal school structure built in Victorian-style architecture. This grand two-story structure became "Oswego Public School." Though it seems a bit foreign for a schoolhouse, Victorian-style architecture was popular in the 1890s. The location of Oswego Public School was about where Lakewood Center stands today. Oswego Public School became Oswego Grammar School, which then became Lakewood School.

Oswego Grammar School was not the only school in town in the early 1900s. Hazelia School—there were three—was named for the hazel brush growing wild in the area. The first schoolhouse was built prior to 1884 near the Emery House off Childs Road on the Shipley donation land claim. In 1884, the second Hazelia school replaced the first one. Also on land donated by A.R. Shipley, it was located on the hill (now Cooks Butte) above the Shipley farm. Hazelia number three was built in 1913 in somewhat the same proximity.

Lucia Bliss taught at Stafford School in 1895. Springbrook

School was on Boones Ferry Road and named for Springbrook Creek that flows into the north side of the lake. Of course, there was also Lake Grove School, located off Boones Ferry Road. Lake Grove Elementary is the largest of Lake Oswego's primary schools. It was rebuilt in 1947 after a fire destroyed the original building.

A labor of love: Lakewood School playground

Lakewood Elementary School's playground was truly a labor of love for the students, parents, and friends of Lakewood whose combined efforts constructed a new playground. Considered the first creation of its kind, the playground was designed by Lake Oswego architect Harold Long and built in the fall of 1974 with under the supervision of retired contractor Virgil White and Pat Nelson's father, the school secretary. John Watts assisted with landscape design. Both Watts and Long had children at Lakewood.

Parents and students also contributed. Eloise Evans and Diane Bradshaw co-chaired the project, which involved two years of fundraising, writing and selling two cookbooks and carnival nights at the school.

On Saturdays, students pitched in to help at the work parties. One Saturday, while digging post holes, a student dug up a toy truck. Diane Bradshaw took charge of the antique relic, which she still has in her possession as of this writing. The author has seen it.

The playground has since been replaced with the new Warner Hall, a rehearsal and practice facility for Lakewood Theatre productions.

Lakewood School, 1940s

Lake Oswego Residents Remember Lakewood School

Julia Marx, a relative of George Rogers, attended Lakewood in the 1930s. She remembers janitor Red McVey yelling at the kids when they were playing outside and it started to rain to "get back in the building!"

Pete Papulski remembers a bomb shelter being built in the early '50s by a group of local fathers. It was dug into the hillside that runs along Greenwood Street. The entrance was located diagonally across from the Methodist Episcopal Church. The shelter had support beams on the top and sides, a gravel floor, and there were bench-type seats for about 20 people.

The Methodist Episcopal Church was originally built in 1894 as Oswego's first church and was where Lakewood Center's Artist Training Facility is now. The church was moved when

Lakewood School was built in 1928. Using ropes and rollers, the church was eased down the embankment—at the edge of Lakewood's parking lot—into a grove of trees on Greenwood Street. The church was used as a theater for the Lake Oswego Community Players.

Mrs. Girod remembers her husband Stan Girod—one of Lakewood's principals—performing the lead role in South Pacific at the Methodist Episcopal Church. (Yes, the one they slid down the hill.) The church served as home to the Lake Oswego Community Players.

Bonnie Hagen Bartnik remembers: "My dad owned Carl's Market, which was across the street from Lakewood. I remember that Nancy Dunis' dad talked my dad into letting me go to a school dance."

Kitchen Counter Drive Saves Tryon

"IT WAS A KITCHEN COUNTER DRIVE because women organized it and weren't afraid to ask for money," proclaimed Lucille (Lu) Beck, referring to the fundraising campaign she spearheaded with close friend Jean Siddall to prevent a housing development in Tryon Creek Park.

During the spring of 1969, Beck became aware that Multnomah County had purchased 45 acres on the Boones Ferry side of Tryon Creek with the vision of creating a large regional park that included a housing development.

Lucille Beck
TRILLIUM TIMES NEWSLETTER

Multnomah County requested a community meeting in June 1969 to discuss this. After the meeting, Beck decided something had to be done to stop the housing development in the park. She and Jean Siddall, a self-trained botanist, organized and became co-chairs of the nonprofit "Friends of Tryon Creek."

Friends of Tryon Creek launched a Kitchen Counter Drive in all the neighboring communities around the Tryon Creek canyon. On April 20, 1970—the first Earth Day—women volunteered to go door to door; school children sold buttons proclaiming, "I am a friend of Tryon Creek." Forest Hills Elementary School, located closest to the park of all the Lake Oswego schools, held a spaghetti dinner, raising $1,200. Within three weeks, 1,400 families donated $27,000 to the cause.

Beck and Siddall approached Glenn Jackson, Chairman of the State Highway Commission, to see if the state could offer financial assistance. At the time, parks fell under the auspices of the Highway Commission. Jackson told the women *no,* but suggested making Tryon a *state* park. Jackson decided within three weeks—by December 1970—to make the whole canyon a state park, and arranged for the purchase of the land.

Lucille Beck graduated from Stanford University, earning a B.A. in Political Science in 1947. She married a Harvard law graduate in 1954 who had recently returned home to the pacific Northwest. A housewife with four children in school, Lu developed an interest in Oregon history and local land and environmental issues, a passion shared by her husband. Lu enjoyed volunteering and spending time exploring the natural canyon between Terwilliger and Boones Ferry Roads. This was pretty much old-horse country. But there was talk of making it a park one day.

That one day came barely a year after Beck and Siddall put their heads together to save Tryon Park. Tryon Creek State Natural Area is Oregon's only state park within a major city.

Rare Plants Were Her Bailiwick

JEANETTE SIDDALL, better known as Jean, moved to Lake Oswego in 1967. She was born June 10, 1930, in Grand Rapids, Michigan and graduated summa cum laude in 1951 from Western Reserve University in Cleveland. She co-organized with Lucille Beck the effort to preserve Tryon Creek as a state park in 1970. She served on the boards of Friends of Tryon Creek, The Nature Conservancy, Oregon Parks Foundation, and Mazamas, a mountaineering organization based in Portland.

In 1974 Jean Siddall received the Aubrey Watzek Award from Lewis & Clark College and a Distinguished Service Award in 1985 from the University of Oregon. She received the Governor's Keep Oregon Livable Award in 1976. She also established the Rare and Endangered Plant Study Center in Lake Oswego, which, of all her life-time accomplishments, is probably her most significant.

Lu Beck and Jean Siddall discussing plans for Tryon Creek State Park

Jean Siddall developed a database of Oregon flora so the information could be used to reconstruct the floristic history and environmental relationships of plants in Oregon. Jean's accumulated data files, maps, punch cards, and reference library were generously donated to Oregon State University's Herbarium for use in research.

In the early 1970s, Jean contacted Kenton Chambers, then-Curator of the Herbarium at OSU, about assembling a comprehensive list of Oregon's rare plant species. Prior to this time, Dr. Chambers had prepared a preliminary list of Oregon rare species, focused especially on endemic taxa. Jean subsequently met with him to add species of her own which she felt were becoming rare through threats from human activities. Their combined preliminary list was used by The Smithsonian Institution in its 1978 publication, *Endangered and Threatened Plants of the United States*.

Jean then acquired a grant from the Fish and Wildlife Service to document information on Oregon's rare species. Of these times, Ken remembers: "Jean was a superb organizer and was the perfect person to lead the cooperative effort that was required in preparing an endangered plant species list for Oregon." Jean set up her central files in a basement office in her home under the organizational title, "Oregon Rare and Endangered Plant Project." Because these were the days before personal computers, the data files all were typed by Jean and her major helpers, one of whom was Sue Vrilakas (now of The Nature Conservancy).

Beginning in 1976, Jean organized the first of four "rare and endangered plant conferences," at which participants responded to a proposed list of Oregon endangered taxa by writing their personal observations about rarity and threats on worksheets. These sheets, plus data from first-hand sighting reports, were transferred by Jean's group of workers to punch cards. Now all such information is kept in computerized databases, like that kept by the Natural Heritage Program, but Jean Siddall and her small corps of workers did it all by hand in the seventies and eighties. Recently, remembering those days, Sue Vrilakas wrote: "Jean had a combination of intelligence, curiosity and focus, topped off with incredible amounts of energy and enthusiasm. She was a person whom it was hard to dissuade but a person who made a difference." Ultimately, Jean's pioneering work led directly to the current Natural Heritage Program and the Oregon Department of Agriculture's rare plant program.

THIRD STOP
NancyWrites (M-Z)

"I hope that when I am gone from here, others will carry on in the same way."
—Mary Goodall

Always Ready for a Fire

Nicknamed "Red" because of his flame-colored hair, Arthur McVey was a jack of all trades and master of most: citizen advocate and preservationist, power-plant construction worker, truant officer for the school board, custodian at Oswego School, active volunteer firefighter—fighting fires was his first love—and secretary of the volunteer firefighter group from 1910 until his death in 1960.

A meeting of Oswego citizens in 1910 at Koehler's Blacksmith Shop organized a-bucket-and-ladder brigade of volunteer fireman consisting of George Miller, first chief, assisted by Edgar Davidson, William Cook, George Prosser, Arthur "Red" McVey, and Earl Hughes. Don Farmer, Bob Montgomery, and Rocky DeBellis also served with McVey as firefighters, but they weren't part of the original five-some.

Neal Cooper comments in Theresa Truchot's *In Their Own Words:* "Red McVey did a wonderful job for years and years as secretary of the volunteer firefighters and he was also a devoted fireman. He had a fire bell in his front yard. His home was located in Old Town near Lakewood School. McVey remained active with the fire department until his death in 1960 at age 83."

During those early years, the original five were no more than a bucket brigade, manning equipment that consisted of twelve leather buckets, two axes, and two 24-foot wooden ladders, one of which hung on the side of the Odd Fellows building in Old Town across from Lakewood School (then Oswego School) for years. The rest of the equipment—such that it was—hung out in the open on poles at 2nd Street and A Avenue.

Rocky DeBellis, longtime friend of McVey's, comments in Truchot's book that Red organized a fundraising drive to purchase an ambulance after G.E. Chaney suffered a heart attack at Al Hughes's service station and it took an ambulance "an hour and a half" to arrive from Portland.

McVey managed to raise $1,000 at the annual Fireman's Ball to purchase a Ford panel truck, which was later traded in for a Cadillac ambulance. The first piece of firefighting equipment that was self-contained and on wheels was a prohibition-confiscated, unclaimed Studebaker sedan, which the volunteer firefighters bought from the city for $1. They converted it into a truck for $555.

"Red" could often be seen walking about town handing out candy to children he passed, his bright red hair disheveled by the wind. When McVey wasn't fighting fires, he worked as a janitor at Lakewood School and served as the citizen watchdog at city council meetings.

Lyle Arthur Baker remembers Red McVey working for the school board as a truant officer. If the kids didn't come to school, he would go out to find out why. "I missed a lot of school between the ages of 6 and 8 because I was a sickly young fellow," states Baker in Truchot's book, "so Red visited our house frequently. Eventually I became well enough to attend school so Red didn't have to make any more visits."

At a City Council meeting on February 8, 1952, then-Mayor Charles Needham declared an official change in street names to honor McVey. The road known as "Old Country Road," which led from Oak Street (in what was then known as New Town) west over the bridge and past the dam to State Street, became McVey Avenue.

"Singin' in the Rain"

Anne Shannon Monroe, great granddaughter of George Shannon, was a local author who lived in Lake Grove, at 16600 Bryant Road. George Shannon, the youngest member of the Lewis and Clark Expedition, was remembered for two things: he got lost on the expedition for two weeks and nearly starved to death; after the expedition he attended law school and served as a senator from Missouri.

Born in Bloomington, Missouri, Anne Shannon moved with her parents and siblings to Yakima, where her father started a medical practice. Dr. Monroe died two years later. The family then moved to Tacoma, where Anne began teaching in 1899. Her aspiration, though, was always to become a writer.

An independent woman even back then, Anne moved from Tacoma to Chicago, where she worked for six years at the *Daily News* as editor of *Common Sense,* a trade magazine. She returned to the West Coast where she ran her own advertising office in Portland from 1907 to 9011. In 1912, New York City beckoned. She began a productive career writing for the *Saturday Evening Post, Good Housekeeping,* and *Ladies Home Journal.* In 1913, Monroe returned to Oregon, settling for a time in Harney County where she managed a 300-acre homestead she purchased for $16.

Monroe wrote fiction, biography, inspirational and self-help books. Her first book, *Eugene Norton: A Tale of the Sagebrush Land* (1900), was published by Rand McNally. One of Monroe's most widely read books was Bill Hanley's autobiography, *Feelin' Fine: Bill Hanley's Book,* for which Monroe was the ghost writer. Hanley was a prominent Harney County rancher who had political aspirations. Monroe's last books, written in 1937 and 1940, were entitled *God Lights A Candle* and *Sparks from Home Fires.*

Anne Shannon Monroe, a quiet, consistent, ambitious, independent woman, never married. A literary voice who lived in Oswego for more than 30 years, the Oregon tales Monroe told were based on her own experiences. Her book, **Singing in the Rain,** is about her brother Reverend Andrew Monroe "whose brave and beautiful life spent carrying the light on the far western frontier was as a continual 'singing in the rain.'" Many of Monroe's books can be found in the Lake Oswego Public Library.

Lover of Trees

AFTER PARKER Farnsworth Morey's death in 1904, his eldest son Frederick decided to sell off parcels of his father's immense estate. He divided the acreage into lots, selling them as part of an area he named "Glenmorrie," in honor of his father (Morrie) and his father's love of trees. (Large stands of trees are often referred to as glens.) Frederick Morey chose the spelling m-o-r-r-i-e instead of m-o-r-e-y because he liked the way it looked in print and he thought that spelling had more charm and appeal for potential buyers.

Parker Farnsworth Morey had no intention of building a residence in the Oswego area because it was too far from his downtown PGE office and his established Portland residence. He merely purchased the land for investment purposes.

The property visible on the right side of this photograph of the Willamette is part of the Parker F. Morey estate.

However, Morey's love of trees and shrubs combined with his love of the peace and quiet nature offers inspired him to begin looking for the "perfect spot" on which to build a grand ranch similar to those of southern plantation owners.

Original Morey house before fire destroyed it

He envisioned an estate planted with acres of fruit and nut orchards suited to Oregon's soil and climate; roadways traversing amongst the foothills to create a park-like setting and native trees...lots of them, as far as the eye could see. According to Herbert Edward Yates, when Morey's estate was completed about 1909, it consisted of some 400 varieties of trees and shrubs, and included a large park with a lake in it where he grew bamboo. Roads and pathways were constructed throughout the acreage and lighted at night with electric bulbs mirrored in reflectors.

Prior to 1890, Morey began buying portions of Felix Collard's donation land claim, part of Jesse Bullock's claim, and part of Gabriel Walling's claim, bits at a time. His entire landholdings extended from where Marylhurst is now, north to Oswego Creek.

A man who loved trees and dedicated himself to buying, planting, and tending them, Morey began his dream project by designing and planting the grounds first, before constructing his dwelling. He persuaded John Gower, head groundskeeper at Stanford University, whom he met while working in California, to move to Oswego to supervise his massive landscaping project from design to installation. Gower, an immigrant from Scotland, jumped at the chance to move to "greener grass."

Gower and Morey worked side by side to create a planting plan consisting of a mix of non-native and native trees which included: Douglas Fir, White Fir, Western Red Cedar, Western Dogwood, Oregon Maple, Hemlock, Port Orford Cedar, and Red Alder. It also included non-natives suggested by Gower: Magnolia, Tamarack, English Holly, Hawthorn, Cryptomeria, Sequoia. The nearby nursery of Walling and Jarisch supplied a great deal of the plant stock.

As the landscape plan was developed and the grounds cleared and tilled, Parker realized that a *large* amount of fertilizer would be needed. He had an idea . . . Powers Brothers Dairy in Fulton Park. He promised them he would "take their entire *accumulation* as soon as he could."

Glenmorrie's distinctive landmark and one of Gower's first suggestions, Poplar Way, is planted with the Lombardy Poplar, imported from France. Poplar Way led from Morey Landing at the junction of Glenmorrie's southern property line and Marylhurst's northern property line. It passed the old mill house which—in 1958—was the only building left of the original ranch properties.

The Camperdownii Elm, another favorite of Gower's and Morey's besides the French poplar, made a wonderful shelter because of its wide overlapping leaves. Under Gower's TLC and expertise, most of the non-natives thrived and can be seen in Glenmorrie today.

Parker Farnsworth Morey—the man who loved trees—served as a harbinger for landscape designers to come. Several of the same trees are planted at the Hoyt Arboretum and many Glenmorrie residents followed Gower's tree-scaping ideas.

Parker Farnsworth Morey died July 7, 1904, from rheumatism, which had crippled him for a good part of his adult life.

The Camperdownii Elm was a favorite of Parker Morey's. Because of its broad overlapping leaves, it made a wonderful shelter from the sun.

STANFORD UNIVERSITY ARCHIVES

Men of Power

E︎DWARD LAWSON EASTHAM, born in 1848 to a Clackamas County family, became a prosperous lawyer. Searching for investments, he purchased the rights to the water works in Walla Walla, Washington. This became a successful business venture by 1883. Eastham returned to Oregon and managed to gain control of the hydroelectric power plant at the falls in Oregon City. He organized the Oregon Falls Electric Company and pioneered the transmission of electric power over long distances in the United States by sending electricity generated at the falls twelve miles to Portland.

PRESERVE OREGON BLOG
[BOTH PHOTOS]

While developing his plan for supplying electric power, Eastham met Parker Farnsworth Morey, a machinist turned mechanical engineer who migrated to Oregon via California from Machias, Maine. On a trip to Portland, Morey discovered that people here could not install hydraulic elevators because the ground was not stable. Morey, inventor and patent-holder that he was, devised a telescoping ramp. His invention became so successful that he remained in Portland and founded the Portland Hydraulic Elevator Company.

Parker F. Morey

Eastham's work with hydroelectric power intrigued Morey financially and mechanically. In 1883, Morey, along with several others, organized the United States Electric Lighting Company of Portland. Formation of United States Electric Lighting Company involved consolidating with Eastham's company.

In 1885, Morey proposed damming the Bull Run River to bring pure drinking water to Portlanders, who were getting eighty percent of their water pumped from the polluted—even back then—Willamette River by Portland Water Company.

Dissatisfaction with Portland Water was rampant. Morey proposed delivering *all* of Portland's water via his elevator company instead of splitting the delivery between his company and Portland Water. A newspaper article carried an article pointing out that Morey's company received $7,200 a year to provide one-fifth of the city's water, while the Portland Water Company received only $3,600 a year for furnishing four-fifths of the water. The article also mentioned that Morey's electric company earned $18,000 a year to furnish the city's lights.

Politicians were skeptical about Morey's proposition because it seemed self-serving, but finally adopted it, only to have legal action strike it down. Although he was disappointed, Parker Morey focused on running his elevator and electric companies.

After Eastham's death in 1891, Morey acquired the assets of the electric company and was elected president. In 1892, he merged United States Electric Lighting Company with General Electric Company of New York. This merger resulted in the formation of Portland General Electric. PGE replaced the conglomeration of his elevator company and Eastham's electric company.

A widower himself, Parker Morey wooed and married Clara Eastham, Edward's widow. Many people say Morey married for money. Parker Morey remained at the helm of PGE until his death in 1904.

NOTE: This article barely scratches the surface of Parker F. Morey's life and accomplishments. If you are interested in a deeper dive, I highly recommend two resources: Theresa Truchot's interview with Herbert Edward Yates in her book, *In Their Own Words* (pp. 128–138), and the *Access Genealogy* website at https://tinyurl.com/bdpmaztu.

Live Where You Play

THE LADD ESTATE Company's well-known advertising slogan, *"Live where you play,"* coined by Vice President Paul Cole Murphy in the 1920s, used Oswego Lake to entice people to buy homes in the newly established Oswego Lake Country Club District.

Paul C. Murphy

Credited with saving Oswego from economic ruin and Oregon Iron and Steel from bankruptcy, Paul C. Murphy, along with Frederick H. Strong, created the Oswego Lake Country Club District between 1923–1925 on the former site of William M. Ladd's Iron Mine Farm, a large dairy farm which sat atop the Prosser iron bed. Mine shafts ran east and west along Country Club Road toward the Willamette River and south to Iron Mountain Road.

In 1923, Murphy joined the Ladd Estate Company as Vice President and general sales manager. Founded by well-known Portland business tycoon and politician William Sargent Ladd, the Ladd Estate Company handled all real estate transactions on behalf of Oregon Iron and Steel. The company's landholdings in Oswego were numerous, especially around the lake. Facing insurmountable debt when the iron furnace shut down, the company decided to focus on developing their real estate assets to generate revenue.

Murphy's vision for Oswego: a booming residential community with the lake as its focal point. He believed Oswego Lake offered a myriad of recreational opportunities not to be found anywhere else, and that outstanding architecture would create a strong community for people who had good taste. Consequently, he solicited the most reputable architects in the Portland area—Wade Pipes, Richard Sundeleaf, Roscoe Hemenway, Morris Whitehouse, Charles Ertz, Van Evera Bailey, and Jamison Parker—to design homes in the Oswego Lake Country Club District and other areas as well.

In surrounding residential districts developed by Murphy and Strong—Forest Hills, Dunthorpe, Riverdale, Riverwood, Palisades—use restrictions and building requirements were imposed to ensure exclusivity. The work of well-known American landscape architect Frederick Law Olmsted, Jr., combined with Arts and Crafts–style architecture and the City Beautiful movement influenced the aesthetics of Murphy's developments.

The City Beautiful movement began in the 1890s with city planners, architects, designers, and landscapers across the nation collaborating to establish a design ethic which would transform American cities—darkened by decades of industrialization and poor, planning—into beautiful places. Frederick Law Olmsted, Jr., and his stepbrother John Charles Olmsted played a key role in the City Beautiful movement. They developed a very complex and comprehensive park plan for Portland, consisting of boulevards, greenways, and parkways, designed to connect various parts of Portland, no matter how far removed.

Both the City Beautiful movement and the architectural trend toward Arts and Crafts–style architecture advocated the use of nature and outdoor recreation as part of the design plan.

By 1926, Murphy and Strong had purchased the Ladd Estate Company, including the extensive landholdings of Oregon Iron and Steel. Murphy eventually bought out Strong's interest and made his son, Paul Fuller Murphy, an officer of the company. Murphy's son worked with his father and carried on the business after his father's retirement in the mid-1940s.

Born in Mount Vernon, Ohio, in 1876, Paul Cole Murphy moved with his family to Washington in 1893 at age 17. Murphy met and married his wife, Mae Fuller, there. Mae gave birth to their only son, Paul Fuller Murphy, five years later.

Prior to becoming a well-known real estate investor, Murphy worked for the City of Everett, Washington, as treasurer. He started developing real estate in Seattle, which he named the Laurelhurst district, with Joseph R. McLaughlin and Frank F. Mead in 1906. Known as The Laurelhurst Company, the partners purchased William S. Ladd's 462-acre Hazel Fern Farm in southeast Portland from the Ladd Estate Company in 1909 for approximately $2 million.

The Laurelhurst Company platted a residential community of about 444 acres in 1,880 lots. They hired the well-known Olmsted Brothers landscape architecture firm to design the neighborhood. By 1916, 500 homes had been built. Because of Murphy's successful Laurelhurst development in Seattle, he reused the name for the Portland neighborhood. During construction, Murphy commuted from Seattle to Portland, residing temporarily at the Portland Hotel. Deciding that commuting wasn't efficient or cost-effective, Murphy moved his family to Portland about 1915. Architects Ellis F. Lawrence and William G. Holford designed Murphy's home in the

Laurelhurst area on East Burnside. The home is listed on the National Register of Historic Places. Murphy served as president of the Portland Realty Board in 1918 and 1919.

Although Murphy's influence on residential development in Lake Oswego was widespread, there isn't a street or neighborhood named after him, unlike Ladd—Ladd's Addition, Ladd's Circle, Ladd Street.

Paul Cole Murphy died September 21, 1957, in Santa Barbara, California, at the age of 81.

NOTE: In 1869, William S. Ladd bought 320 acres of land from the Thomas Frazer Hazelwood Farm in southeast Portland. Ladd made subsequent purchases of additional properties in 1873 and 1876. He also purchased property from Louis Marier. This collection of properties became the Hazel Fern Farm—one of three farms owned completely by Ladd. Ladd also owned five other farms with Simeon G. Reed.

Central park in Ladd's Addition
OREGON HISTORICAL SOCIETY RESEARCH LIBRARY

A Flavorite Spot

HOME-MADE... BY HAND... all 24 flavors. There was nothing like Newton's 24 Flavors for a dip, a scoop, a Flaming Snowball, a Twofer, or a special order. Opened originally as Rose's 24 Flavors, the shop was located at 39 B Avenue—the space vacated by Gourmet Productions. Owners Rose Larsen and Harry Hansen sold the shop to Oran "Newt" Newton in November 1958.

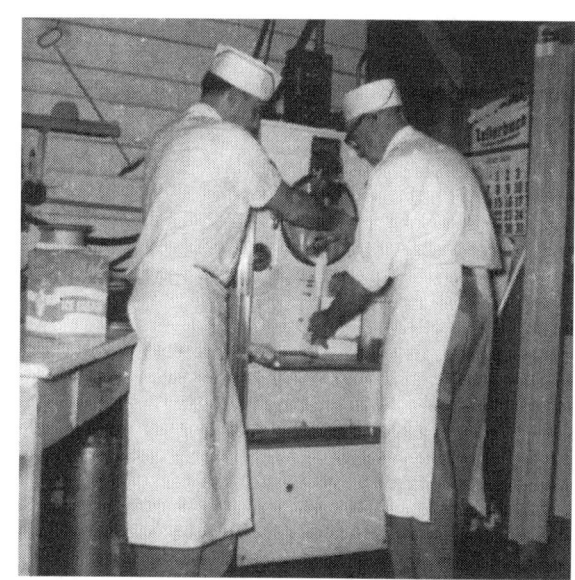

Grandpa Newton & his son Oran making ice cream

Although he came from the corporate world of Safeway, Newt earned his degree in food technology from Oregon State and had always dreamed of having his own business. When his sister-in-law called to tell him Rose's 24 Flavors was for sale, "Dad almost had us moved the next day," remembers Jan. What a stroke of luck ... something more closely related to his college degree *and* his own business! For 20 years, Newt, his wife Maxine, daughter Janice and son Tom, occasionally Aunt Thelma, and Grandpa Newton could all be found working in the "deep freeze" at various times. It was a family affair. (Dot connection:

Third Stop: Nancy Writes (articles M–Z) • 93

Jan and the author and Jan's husband Ken Becker were all high school chums. The Beckers currently live on a farm in West Linn.)

When Oran Newton first bought the shop, ice cream was the only thing on the menu. "Sandwiches and soup were added, along with salads and other delicacies like Mom's Walnut Squares and her three bean salad. We became a full-fledged sandwich shop in 1965," remembers Jan, "well known for our tongue-tingling chili, the three-beaner salad, and of course, ice cream." (These recipes can be found in the *Cooking Up Oswego Memories Cookbook* available at Oswego Heritage House and Museum.)

Jan's dad always used to joke that his ice cream parlor was the inspiration for Farrell's because he was here first. It did kind of remind me of Farrell's without all the dinging and donging and the flying carpet of ice cream zooming around the room above your head. Newton's had a similar ambiance to Farrell's—red-flocked wall paper, small round tables, wire-backed ice cream parlor chairs—you know the ones—a juke box and a popcorn machine. The place was filled with people of all ages chattering and laughing, singing "Happy Birthday" or hanging out after a football game or a school dance. Tom and Jan chuckle as they tell me that the aftermath of having a hoard of junior high school kids drop in after a dance was always an interesting cleanup experience.

Ice cream definitely was Newton's specialty. Many of the recipes were handed down from Rose Larsen and then tweaked and new ideas for flavors emerged. Newton's offered ice cream in standard flavors, but they also made ice cream to coincide with the changing seasons. Both Jan and Tom remember peeling peaches—and the aroma that created—for the peach ice cream, a summertime-only offering. Root beer was another summertime flavorite, as was Cherry Berry. In January and February cherry ice cream was served up in honor of the presidents' birthdays. Newton's could create or concoct any flavor for any occasion.

"Cherry Berry got its name," Jan recalls, "because Grandpa Newton, who often helped out with the ice cream making, accidently mixed cherry flavoring into the strawberry ice cream or strawberry flavoring into the cherry. I can't remember which. We decided to call it Cherry Berry. People loved it."

Tom tells the story of Newton's being asked to make 500 Flaming Snowballs for an event at the convention center when Gerald Ford was in town. He says the logistics of making 500 snowballs; delivering them, and keeping them cold was definitely a challenge. Jan remembers a story about a woman who wanted us to make cinnamon-flavored ice cream; and then there was the special order one Christmas for a crème de menthe ice cream pie. "We weren't supposed to serve liquor, but Dad did the pie anyway... for several years."

More fond memories of growing up in the freezer from Jan and Tom: "We used to hire boys with bicycles during the summer to deliver our homemade ice cream sandwiches. They kept the ice cream sandwiches cold on dry ice that they carried in baskets attached to their bikes. They would ride around the neighborhoods dinging their bells selling our ice cream treats. Twofers were a high-demand item, especially the dipped ones.

You could have one side dipped or both sides dipped into any number of sprinkles, candies, etc. Especially popular was the Freckle Twofer—two different flavors dipped in chocolate sprinkles."

Not related to ice cream, but relating to the Newton family are the dot connections to the pioneer Bickner family. Across the street from the ice cream parlor (where Rite Aid is) lived John Bickner, one of the Bickner boys—son of Joseph A. Bickner who owned a grocery in town on State Street. Grandpa Newton used to shop at Bickner's Grocery.

According to Jan's mother, John visited Newton's Ice Cream Parlor frequently . . . so frequently that he felt compelled to give the Newtons a family heirloom wind-up clock, complete with original oil and key. Jan's mom gave the clock to Jan, who donated it to the Oswego Heritage House and Museum. Recently Jan told me her grandmother bought 65 pieces of crystal from John Bickner as a wedding present for her and Ken.

Back to ice cream: What is *your* favorite flavor? Jan's—licorice; Tom's—opera house fudge; mine—chocolate peanut butter fudge.

Cementing Oswego's Future

"PORTLAND CEMENT to be manufactured in Oswego, Oregon" announced the *Morning Oregonian* August 2, 1908. The town buzzed with excitement. This was Oswego's first new industry in over 20 years, and the only manufacturer of cement in Oregon.

C.W. Nibley of Salt Lake City, president of a large cement company in Utah, headed up the development of the new plant, located in what is now the Foothills area of Lake Oswego. Like the decision makers of Oregon Iron and Steel, he selected Oswego for the location of the manufacturing plant. It was close to the Willamette where rail and river transportation were available. Raw materials came from the towns of Roseburg, Rufus, and Dallas, Oregon. Portland Cement Company incorporated in 1909; construction began in 1910. But it wasn't until 1916 that cement was first produced.

Financial difficulties plagued the operation, with many of Portland's Commercial Club investors threatening to withdraw their money. Robert Pim Butchart, of Butchart Garden fame in Victoria, British Columbia, came to the rescue in 1915. Butchart, who owned several successful cement plants in Canada, joined forces with Charles Boettcher of Denver, owner of several successful cement plants in the Midwest. Together they reorganized the company's financial structure, changed the name to Oregon Portland Cement Company, and rebranded the original product from Red Rose to Oregon Portland Cement.

Butchart hired fellow Canadian Lawrence Newlands as plant superintendent. Newlands was civic minded and offered the plant's clubhouse to the public for community meetings. Next to the clubhouse was a baseball diamond used by the company's Oswego team. Both were located where Whole Foods 365 is now. Previously the building housed the Dahl restaurant, Chapel by the Lake mortuary, and Albertsons.

Sales were slow at first, but sound financial footing and strong leadership guided the company to success—so successful that in 1923 Butchart decided to build another plant in Lime, Oregon, known as Sun Portland Cement Company. Sun Portland Cement and Oregon Portland Cement merged in 1926.

Contrary to popular perception, Oregon Portland Cement Company and Oregon Portland Cement were not named for Portland, Oregon. A bricklayer from England developed, patented, and named the cement Portland because the color of concrete made from his cement reminded him of a white-gray limestone quarried on the Isle of Portland in Dorset, England, and he wanted a name that distinguished his cement from other cements.

Although Oregon Portland Cement Company ceased production in 1981 and the plant was demolished in 1987, memories and relics remain. Bits of the old plant, parts of an old elevator used to lower a 988 Caterpillar front-end loader, and part of the old crusher building, now the base of a deck at Oswego Pointe, can be seen at the north dolphin piers on the Willamette in Foothills Park.

Patrick Bloedorn, a packing house lead man, wrote in the *Lake Oswego Review* (July 28, 2011), "I remember walking north

Oregon Portland Cement

from the number one packing house along the lower railroad tracks towards Foothills Road to pick up paperwork from the lime department, which took me through the old, abandoned part of the cement plant. On my left at night in the pouring rain would be the number one kiln, shut down for years and rusting in the damp.

"On my right side would be the old finish grind. Old ball mills covered in moss had been silenced for years. Above the old ball mills were two giant steel hoppers, two stories tall. When they shut them down for the last time they left them full of clinker and gypsum. Long stalactites hung down, formed by dripping water, giving it a very spooky look at night. I could almost feel the spirits of the men who were killed or injured there. I raise my whiskey glass and give those old guys a toast. They got the job done. OPC shipped out over half a million tons of cement in a year."

Linus Pauling remembers spending countless hours at the cement plant when he was in his early teens. "My grandparents lived on 4th Street in Oswego. Whenever I went to visit, I would walk over to the cement company laboratories and bombard the chief chemist with all kinds of questions."

Motivated by his early contact with the chemist and his need to earn money, Pauling took a summer job in southern Oregon as a blacktop pavement inspector. His task was to monitor the quality of the bitumen-stone mixes comprising the pavement. His activities were published in "The Manufacture of Cement in Oregon," which appeared in *The Student Engineer* in June 1920. Pauling specified the process by which cement was produced, from crushers cutting large rocks as a first step to the kilns yielding the final, small round particles for cooling in the finishing mill.

Oregon Portland Cement made many significant contributions to Oswego and nearby towns: the building of the Oregon City elevator, the locks at Oregon City Falls, the old West Linn/Oregon City bridge, the Abernethy Bridge, most of the bridges in downtown Portland, the Federal Building on SW 2nd Ave. and SW Madison. Also on the list: a good part of the dams on the Columbia River; countless homes in Portland and Vancouver, Washington; the number-two powerhouse at Bonneville; and the Glenn Jackson Bridge.

Dig, Dug, Done

TUALATIN RIVER Navigation and Manufacturing Co. (TRNM) organized in 1864 for the purpose of creating a continuous waterway between the Tualatin Valley and Portland, making Oswego a major shipping center for transporting Tualatin Valley crops and lumber.

To create a continuous waterway from Tualatin Valley to Portland, TRNM needed two canals. One would replace the horse-drawn railroad between the Tualatin and the west end of Sucker Lake. After passing through that canal, a steamer would transport logs and produce over Sucker Lake. The cargo would then travel through a second canal and on to Portland.

Headgate at confluence of Oswego Canal and Tualatin River

The second canal, to be dug at the east end of Sucker Lake where it spills into the Willamette, would replace the portage on Sucker Creek's north side, requiring locks due to the major difference in water levels. Albert Durham and

John Trullinger used to carry lumber an eighth of a mile from their sawmill to Oswego Landing, where the original portage was. The idea of a second canal was abandoned in 1873 when completion of Willamette Falls Locks made traffic past the Falls possible without portage.

Following are some key dates in Oswego Canal's history:

- 1869 TRNM stockholder and riverboat captain John Kellogg builds a steamer to run on Sucker Lake. The plan was to connect this vessel with the sternwheeler *Onward*, also built by Kellogg, that ran on the Tualatin.

- 1871 George Low Curry, president of TRNM, digs the first shovel of dirt for the Oswego Canal.

    Chinese laborers from TRNM hewed solid rock to construct the canal. The company also built a dam to raise the level of the water to make it more navigable. The dam created the first expansion of the lake from 2.75 miles to 3.5 miles. The canal reestablished the connection between the Tualatin River and Sucker Lake that ancient volcanic activity destroyed.

- 1872 Oswego Canal is completed but not navigable until January of 1873 due to low water.

- 1873 Sternwheeler *Onward* makes the first passage down Oswego Canal.

- 1880 Oregon Iron and Steel takes possession of Oswego Canal from Tualatin River Navigation and Manufacturing.

- 1881 Oswego Canal is widened to increase water pressure.

1913 Sucker Lake officially becomes Oswego Lake.

1928 Canal is dug to connect Oswego Lake to the Duck Pond. The Duck Pond was originally a marshy area adjacent to the main lake to the east which flooded. The canal allowed the Duck Pond to become part of Oswego Lake. It eventually became Lakewood Bay and allowed for more real estate development around the lake.

Oswego Heritage House & Museum

Designed by Charles Ertz and built in 1928, the "big white house" at the top of A Avenue and 10th Street served as the office for the Ladd Estate Company real estate business headed by Paul C. Murphy, Vice President and General Sales Manager.

Oswego Heritage House

The original structure—documented as the Ladd Estate Company Forest Hills Branch Office on the Oregon Inventory of Historic Properties held by the City of Lake Oswego's Historic Resources Advisory Board—consisted of two offices and a parlor. Also known as the Murphy Building, the structure is located in the path of an old mine trail on Iron Mountain known as the Prosser Mines, which carried iron ore from the mines to the smelter near present-day Rogers Park. Murphy positioned the building so he could have a view from the front windows looking down A Avenue toward Mt. Hood in the background.

Dr. William Cane and his wife Winifred bought the Murphy Building in 1939, remodeling and expanding it so it could be used for both their residence and his medical practice. When Dr. Cane's wife passed away in February of 1996, he moved into a retirement home. The home remained vacant and fell into disrepair, needing a great deal of renovation, when

Bill Headlee, a member of the Oswego Heritage Council, purchased it in 1997, with the intention of making the building a permanent home for the Oswego Heritage Council. According to Herald Campbell, the grounds around the building had become so overgrown only the top of the house could be seen from A Avenue.

The Oswego Heritage Council hired contractor Bill Oyalla to do the renovations. He restored the three original rooms, adding an exhibit space, meeting room, and kitchen. Bill Gerber designed the landscape. The Oswego Heritage Council opened the doors of the Oswego Heritage House and Museum's permanent home in 1999. The historic building is on the City of Lake Oswego's Landmark Designation List.

From 1970 until 1999, the Oswego Heritage Council operated without a permanent home, meeting in various locations around the city. Programs in the early years consisted of placing historic landmark plaques around town, providing programs for elementary schools, lectures, and whatever else the Heritage Council board felt needed support.

Now officially named the Oswego Heritage House and Museum, the building serves as a historic resource and community gathering place for special events, various and sundry meetings, First Wednesday Chautauqua lectures, and headquarters for the Classic Car and Boat Show. The museum features a permanent exhibit showcasing Oswego's early Native Americans. Personal photos and letters from some of Oswego's descendants and early pioneer families tell the intimate stories of life in Oswego from the 1850s to the early 1960s. Rotating special exhibits with a history-specific theme such as schools, commerce, and women's suffrage are also part of the museum's offerings.

In the comfortable parlor library, magazines, books, and other reading material are available to the public for on-site perusal. A computer linking to the Lake Oswego Public Library's Digital History Collection is also available for on-site use.

Dr. Mark Browne heads up the archive department at the Oswego Heritage House and Museum. He is available for consultations to those wanting assistance and guidance about how and where to preserve family history such as heirlooms, artifacts, photos, journals, etc. To arrange an appointment with Dr. Browne: mcbdds@sbcglobal.net. For general information about the museum, building rental, and Heritage Council membership, visit https://www.oswegoheritage.org.

Gertrude Thacker, Kenny Burdick, Mary Goodall

Third graders ignite inspiration for historical societies

"Here's a dollar for the museum," Forest Hills third-grader Robert Landers told his teacher Gertrude Thacker in 1964 after hearing local historian and author Theresa Truchot talk to his class.

Truchot talked to the students about her book, *Charcoal Wagon Boy*, explaining what a charcoal wagon boy was, why they were important, and showing artifacts she had collected. She told the class, "Wouldn't it be wonderful to have a museum for my collection so lots of people can see it and I wouldn't have to store it in various garages or drive it around? Phyllis Miska stated in an oral history interview with Theresa Truchot (*In Their Own Words*), "It's a great deal of work to carry the artifacts around to different places, so we are hoping for a permanent home for them very soon."

Little did Truchot know the impact that statement and her talk would have. Nickels, dimes, and pennies came trickling in from students, parents, and the community at large. Thacker didn't know what to do, since it was against school policy to collect money. Thacker, Principal Maynard Christianson, and Truchot discussed the situation, finally deciding a little historical group be organized in Thacker's classroom with the understanding that the group was not sanctioned by the school district and was not part of district curriculum.

Her class organized the first—and only—Junior Historical Society in Oregon. Officers elected were students Rob Beadle, President, Barbara Bailey, secretary, Pamela Miska, treasurer.

The first three volunteer Moms for this first group were Phyllis Miska, Rob Beadle's mother and Jerome Grant's mother; Advisors were Mary Goodall, Sally Harding, Theresa Truchot, and Gertrude Thacker. The idea of a historical society organized by individual teachers and classrooms started to catch on in other schools: Mrs. Thurlow's class at Uplands Elementary followed Gertrude Thacker; then Mrs. Phyllis Carr's class at Bryant Elementary.

Activities of the historical societies included having garage sales to raise money for a museum; selling stationary cards designed by Theresa Truchot of the furnace; creating a historic mural for their schools; bus tours around Oswego given by Forest Hills bus driver Edna Farmer in "her" school bus; caring for the Odd Fellows Pioneer Cemetery on Stafford Road (now

Oswego Pioneer Cemetery); setting up displays around town of Truchot's—and then Mary Goodall's—collection of artifacts.

Mary Goodall organized the first community display in the Shon-Tay office building in Lake Grove off Boones Ferry Road. She donated the use of one room on the main floor to be used as a "museum." Although the exhibit showcased a collection of artifacts and an exhibit of animals related to the history of Oswego as researched by Gene Smith, the *really big draws* were Mr. Duis' police dog and Mary Strong's dog, who always slept under the table at the old library in city hall.

The idea of forming historical societies within individual classrooms grew so quickly that within two years they had become a district-wide phenomenon among students, parents, faculty, and the community. However, managing all the various groups at the different schools created a challenge. A district society was formed, but it was difficult to pull together because the schools were so spread out. The district society decided to operate independently from the schools, but eventually disbanded. As quickly as the societies sprung up, they dissolved due to lack of cohesiveness.

However, Mary Goodall was able to keep the fire stoked. Interest in local history was at an all-time high—because of the kids' historical societies; the publication of Theresa Truchot's book, *In Their Own Words*; and the celebration of Oswego's 100-year anniversary—and Goodall did not want the historic J.R. Irving farmhouse on Boones Ferry Road built in 1870 demolished to make way for a shopping center.

Goodall worked tirelessly finding other like-minded individuals who were interested in preserving the history and beauty of the home, but in the end Mountain Park shopping center replaced the Irving farmhouse. Community leaders like Bill Headlee, George Bergeron, Herald Campbell, Bill Gerber, Bill Warner, members of Lake Oswego Rotary, Lake Oswego Chamber members, Phyllis Miska, Theresa Truchot and many many others supported Goodall and her efforts to preserve the history and beauty of the home. These men and women joined together to form the Oswego Heritage Council. Although they were not able to save the Irving farmhouse, the Oswego Heritage Council continues with its mission to preserve Oswego's historical heritage.

A Plot with a View

JESSE BULLOCK and Nancy Howard Bullock lost their 20-year-old son not long after arriving in Oswego. They had no decent place to bury him so they created a plot on part of their donation land claim. One plot became two, then three, four and so on, as other deaths followed. This continual development and addition of plots led the Bullocks to donate five acres of their 618-acre donation land claim to establish a family cemetery between 1850 and 1881.

Their donation land claim extended from Oswego Pioneer Cemetery and ran along Stafford Road—known as Market Road in the 1800s—to Marylhurst, where the original Christie School was constructed. Farmers used Market Road to transport goods to Portland. Portland businessman, politician, and postmaster George Steel named the Stafford area—and Stafford Road—after his hometown of Stafford, Ohio.

Sometime between 1871 and 1873, Jesse and Nancy Bullock's daughter, Lucy Bullock, married George Prosser, becoming his second wife. Jesse Bullock and his son-in-law George Prosser expanded the cemetery in 1881 to include other families. The Bullock-Prosser families donated the cemetery in 1892 to Oregon Iron and Steel (OIS) for the company to use as a final resting place for its employees. OIS had owned the title to the cemetery for 42 years when the Methodist Episcopal Church took possession in 1934. Ownership transferred again in 1938 to the Odd Fellows Lodge. For the next 40 years it was known as the "Odd Fellows Cemetery."

George Prosser was an active member of the Odd Fellows Lodge, whose main function was to care for the deceased. Prosser and several other Odd Fellows attended to the burial of members' families, making arrangements for funerals and visiting the mourners.

The entire Bullock and Prosser families are buried at Oswego Pioneer Cemetery. By the 1960s, the cemetery was nothing but a mass of overgrown brush, a web of weeds covering the grave markers, many of which had been damaged by weather. Herbert Nelson, a friend of the Prosser family, recalled being contacted in 1973 by Sylver Prosser, one of George's daughters, who lived in Pasadena, California. "She wanted to know if I would take care of all the Prosser family graves. I told her I would and have ever since. The first time I went up there I couldn't drive my car to the plots. The grass was so tall and wet and slippery that my wheels kept spinning. I left my car and walked up there. I had gone up there a week before and cleaned the blackberry briars that was growing up all over the place."

The 1970s saw a change thanks to Ethel Schaubel and Bill Blizzard, then-owner of the *Lake Oswego Review*. They garnered support from a group of concerned citizens to restore the site and incorporate the cemetery.

Oswego Pioneer Cemetery incorporated in 1977 and the cemetery was designated by the City of Lake Oswego as an Historic Landmark in 1989. Today, Oswego Pioneer Cemetery is a nonprofit 501(c)(3) corporation operated by a volunteer board.

Over 90 iron workers from OIS are buried at Oswego Pioneer Cemetery and the adjacent Sacred Heart Cemetery. Linus Pauling, his wife Ava Helen Miller, and Pauling's grandfather Charles are buried in the cemetery as are three more generations of the Pauling family. Other notables buried at Oswego Pioneer Cemetery include Adam Shipley and his wife Celinda, James and Susie Cook, nine Oswego mayors, six town marshals, and 117 war veterans who served from the American Civil War to the Iraq War.

If you are interested in knowing who is buried at Oswego Pioneer Cemetery, the OPC board has compiled a comprehensive list of names through 2016; really interesting to peruse, if you are so inclined. Please contact the author if you would like a copy: nancy@thehistoricconnection.com.

NOTE: William S. Ladd, president of Ladd & Tilton Bank and one of the primary investors in Oregon Iron and Steel, founded River View Cemetery in 1882. Apparently he wanted a cemetery for the financially well-off. Oswego Pioneer Cemetery was for the working class.

Guardian Angel of Oswego Pioneer Cemetery

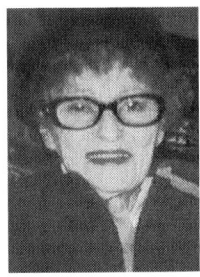

Ethel Schaubel

"I FOUND MY MAN," Ethel Schaubel exclaimed after discovering Richard Santee loved old cemeteries as much as she did. Schaubel invited Santee to lunch and the next thing he knew she had persuaded him to take over management of Oswego Pioneer Cemetery. Santee recollected, "I had just returned to the Oswego area after retiring from the University of California, Berkeley, as an administrator and sociology professor. Now I'm running a cemetery."

When she was a youngster, Schaubel's parents, Nina Worthington and James Peter Emmott, tended the family graves at Oswego Pioneer Cemetery along with many of the townspeople. However, the practice went by the wayside when Schaubel and her husband moved to Hawaii to open one of the first car rental companies there.

Upon her return to her hometown of Oswego in 1949, Schaubel visited the cemetery. Dismayed to see her mother's severly weather-damaged gravestone, knee-high weeds, and unkept shrubbery all around—some of which had been planted by early area residents—Schaubel knew she had to take action. The cemetery needed a manager.

When Schaubel wasn't cleaning up the five-acre cemetery with friends and family members, "she operated a beauty salon—The Bob Shop—in downtown Lake Oswego," recalled Nancy

Headlee, president of the Oswego Pioneer Cemetery Board that continues Schaubel's work.

Schaubel had many plans for the cemetery, which was platted in 1881 by George W. Prosser. One goal was to create a map showing the plots of the more than 1,200 individuals buried there.

Working with his brother-in-law, Steve Dietz, Santee modernized the cemetery filing system, which had resided in cardboard boxes. With the help of Nancy Headlee, he established a board for what is now a nonprofit organization. For more details about the history of the cemetery, early area settlers, and directions for finding graves contact the author at nancy@thehistoricconnection.com.

Another Schaubel goal was to hire a resident caretaker to deter vandalism and help with upkeep. That goal was fulfilled when a house was moved from the city's First Addition to the cemetery.

For more than 25 years, Jerry Instenes, who repaired machinery by day and was a city police officer by night, volunteered at the cemetery. "That began," he said, "when I repaired the cemetery's riding mower and observed the sloppy work done by the young people who had been running the machinery. Ethel asked me if I could do the mowing until she found someone permanently. That was 28 years ago," Instenes laughed.

Now retired, Officer Instenes said he was happy to turn the mowing over to Joe Collins, a retired city employee, who became the cemetery's caretaker—a paid position. Instenes remains a cemetery volunteer, helping families select plots for loved ones. He described Schaubel as "a dear friend to me.... However, when it came to reclaiming and improving the historic burial ground," he said, "she was tough as nails."

In years past, Schaubel worked daily in the cemetery from March to Memorial Day. On Memorial Day weekend, she instructed volunteers to get the names and addresses of visitors and, with luck, a donation to help with the cemetery work. Some of the graves she reclaimed from overgrowth bear familiar names such as Borland, Bullock, Dyer, Freepons, Hallinan, Shipley, Walling, Wanker, Worthington.

Born in Lake Oswego in 1920, Ethel Schaubel died April 17, 2014, at the age of 93, at the home of her son Ian Elliot in Ellensburg, Washington.

Electricity Comes to Town

BUILT BY Oregon Iron and Steel (OIS) in 1909, Oswego's power plant was the brainchild of OIS shareholders as a means to several ends: generate electricity for the iron pipe and foundry business; resell electricity to improve cash flow; and maintain their water rights. The company owned the Sucker Creek dam and Sucker Lake water rights; but in order to retain those rights, the water had to be used for industrial purposes. With the cessation of iron production in 1894, and commerce almost at a standstill, those rights were in jeopardy of being lost.

Nathanial S. Keith was hired to investigate how feasible it would be to build a power plant in Oswego. A well-known electricity expert from New York, Keith gave Oswego high marks as a location for a power plant, which became known as Oswego Hydro. Now just referred to as the power plant, it is owned and operated by the Lake Oswego Corporation, as are the dam and head gate.

Oswego power plant

A dam located at the east end of Oswego Lake controls the flow of water from the lake into the Willamette River. Some of the water is diverted into a power plant, via a large penstock—an enormous circular pipe used to carry water to a turbine—where electricity is generated. A head gate located off Childs

Road, not easily visible, controls the flow of water from the Tualatin River into Oswego Lake, via a canal.

The power plant is located just below the McVey Bridge. Looking at the very square concrete building, you would never guess that inside is a massive turbine—a Westinghouse horizontal water turbine with a 48-inch Francis, double-cupped water wheel mounted on a 7-inch continuous shaft, to be exact. The manufacturer design plate reads "patent dates 1895–1905, 500 KVA unit, 2400 volt, 360 RPM and a 700 horsepower rated generator."

This original Westinghouse turbine is operational today. However, it requires people with the mechanical knowledge and technical skill to maintain and repair this particular turbine. During the 1950s and '60s, this was not a problem. A handful of people could be called upon. But as of 2015, only one of that select group is still around: Stuart Dunis, brother of the author. He worked for the Lake Oswego Corporation for 16 years, spending many hours servicing the turbine. One year, Dunis had to make a special part for the dinosaur turbine while waiting for the one he ordered to arrive, just so the power plant could resume generating electricity quickly.

Dunis recalls that, early on, full-time operators were needed to physically man the turbine from 6:00 A.M. to 10:00 P.M., seven days a week. Following is a list of names of dedicated individuals who worked as operators, transmission line servicers, and repair and maintenance technicians over the years.

1925–1930   P.M. Brumbaugh

1928–1933   E. Wing

1934–1936   F. Rose

1936–1938   Griffin

1950–1955   Cowles, Parker, Wright

(After 1955, it was no longer necessary to man Oswego Hydro 24/7 but twice daily checks were still being done.)

1955–1964   C. Trainer, R. DeBellis (Dot connection: daughters of Trainer and DeBellis were in my class.)

1964–1968   C. Davidson

1973–1986   Wilson, Graham, Kern

1986–2003   C. Schaeffer

1987–2003   S. Dunis

Others who made it possible for the 1905 hydro unit to stay on line included Carl Halvorson, developer of Mountain Park (dot connection: Halvorson's daughter was another classmate of mine); M. McCarty, a machinist; L. Fisher, a BPA engineer; and S. Henderson, a machinist and inventor.

Electrician Bill Banks worked at Oswego Hydro in the 1920s. He recalls (in *In Their Own Words* by Theresa Truchot): "One particular night, the doors wide open, a logging truck had just gone by, and shortly afterwards I heard this groanin' sound. It went on for hours until daylight. Then daylight came and I spoke to my relief operator, 'It sounded like somebody had been hit by that logging train from all the groaning that was going on.' 'Oh, those are just bull frogs out in the swamp.'" During his shift, Banks would sit in front of a pot-bellied stove to keep warm. Dunis says you can see the spot in the wall where the pipe from the stove carried the smoke to the outside.

Oswego first became "electrified" in 1910, generating electricity for household use.

Many people think the lake is man made. The original lake is not; it resulted from the Missoula floods at the end of the ice age. Over the years, however, man has changed the shoreline, the depth, and the water level of the lake.

The First Ore Mined in Oswego

ONE OF THE ORIGINAL investors in Oregon Iron and Steel Company, Matthew Patton was born in Monongahela County, Virginia, in 1805. Prior to coming to Oregon, he lived and worked in Indiana, Ohio, Illinois, and Missouri.

Patton became an apprentice to Eli Collins, a cabinet maker. After applying himself diligently for four years, Patton started his own furniture business in Lafayette, Indiana. There he met Catherine Grimes, whom he married in 1830. Due to the limited demand for furniture, Patton moved to Frankfort, Indiana, where he established himself as a general merchandise proprietor. From there he moved to Missouri, where he founded the city of Pattonsburg. He made his home there until 1847, building a saw and grist mill.

Matthew Patton

Hearing of the potential discovery of iron ore in Oregon, and the discovery of gold in California, Patton packed up his wife and five children and embarked for the land of opportunity in a prairie schooner. Patton brought with him 70 head of cattle, 300 sheep, and 3 horses. After a long and tedious journey across wilderness and desert, the family arrived at The Dalles.

Since there was no practical way to get from The Dalles to Portland at the time, a flatboat was constructed, using trees in the area and launched into the Columbia River with the women and children of the Patton and Carter families aboard. When the boat reached Cascade Falls, the men hired Native Americans to guide the women and children through rugged terrain and swift-running streams, seven miles downsteam to the Lower Cascades. Several of the men drove the animals by land to the Lower Cascades. Those not driving animals rode the boat over the dangerous rapids with the Native Americans. Miraculously, everyone made it without incident.

Although the Patton party experienced many hardships during this tedious and strenuous journey, they finally arrived somewhere close to Fort Vancouver, where they headed south into the Willamette Valley. Patton selected a location in the Chehalem Valley for his family home.

However, he was off again when the gold fever struck. After six weeks of mining and $5,000 in his pocket, Patton headed home on the boat *Undine.* He encountered misfortune when the drunken *Undine* captain went into Shoalwater Bay instead of the mouth of the Columbia, leaving Patton to walk the rest of the way.

Matthew Patton used a portion of his money to purchase part of the Collard donation land claim in the late 1850s. It lay south of Sucker Creek, but the vein extended north into the hills now known as Iron Mountain. Here he "strip mined" the first iron ore to be smelted at Oregon Iron Works—which became Oregon Iron and Steel. Strip mining is the process of removing a long strip of overlying soil and rock before the ore is removed.

Patton and his wife platted South Oswego in 1883. Consisting of only a few streets, those running east and west were named First through Fourth. The lots were laid out in a grid system, which wasn't well suited to the hilly terrain. Development concentrated around Third Street (Oak Street), the only improved road in the area at the time. However, the banner year of 1890 in the iron industry spurred growth, and Patton's son and his partners established "South Oswego Addition" one year later. In the process, the original numbered streets were changed to names of species of trees—Laurel, Oak, Ash.

Patton Road in Lake Oswego and Patton Road in the west hills on Council Crest are both named after Matthew Patton.

Yes, Virginia, Linus Pauling Spent Time in Oswego

Linus and Ava Pauling
THE LINUS PAULING INSTITUTE

Dr. Linus Pauling and his wife Ava Helen were remarkable human beings, together and individually. One of the world's greatest scientists, humanitarian, and defender of civil liberties, Dr. Pauling is buried in Oswego Pioneer Cemetery; Ava Helen Miller, his wife, is buried next to him. Many of Pauling's relatives are also buried there.

Although he was born in Portland in 1901, Linus Pauling spent summers in Lake Oswego with his grandparents, who lived on 4th Street. He remembers spending countless hours at the cement plant when he was in his early teens. "I would walk over to the cement company laboratories and bombard the chief chemist with all kinds of questions."

Pauling received his Bachelor's degree in chemical engineering in 1922 from Oregon Agricultural College in Corvallis—now Oregon State University (OSU). He attended Caltech for post-graduate study, receiving a Ph.D. in chemistry and mathematical physics in 1925. He joined the Caltech faculty in the fall of 1927.

Born in Beavercreek in 1903, Ava Helen Miller grew up in Salem. Like Linus, she also attended OSU. She had enrolled in a course titled "Chemistry for Home Economics Majors." He was teaching the course. When they met—to quote a line from the *Hart to Hart* TV series starring Stephanie Powers and Robert Wagner—"it was murder." Or should I say it was chemistry, all right. They married in 1923.

Ava, well known as a peace rights activist, introduced Linus to the field of peace studies for which he received the Nobel Peace Prize in 1962. He used to say it was really Ava who should have won the peace prize, or at least it should have been shared. He won his first Nobel Prize in 1954 in Chemistry and is the only person to receive two unshared Nobel Prizes. Dr. Pauling founded the Linus Pauling Institute; has over 1,000 publications to his name, and has received numerous additional awards and commendations—too many to list here.

Not only was Ava an active peace rights supporter, but also a supporter of women's rights. American politics and social reform also interested her. The main thrust of her activities centered around her concern for human beings. Together she and Linus campaigned to stop the production and use of nuclear arms. Their campaigning led to the Limited Test Ban Treaty between the United States and the Soviet Union, effectively ending the above-ground testing of nuclear weapons.

Ava and Linus raised four children. She continually worked to maintain a home environment which would allow her husband to continue his scientific work without the distractions of family life.

A *Leafing* Legacy

"I WOULD VENTURE TO SAY that 90 percent of the trees and shrubs planted in the old part of Lake Oswego came from J.B. Pilkington Nursery" states Esther Pilkington, wife of nurseryman Clarke Pilkington. "There is a huge cut-leaf Japanese maple growing near the corner of B and 2nd Street that Dr. Pilkington imported from Japan more than 80 years ago."

The legacy left by the Pilkington Family—Dr. John Pilkington, his son John, Jr., John Jr.'s son Clarke and his wife Esther—can be seen in many parts of Portland and Lake Oswego. Pilkington Road is named for the family nursery business, J.B. Pilkington Nursery, which for 40 years was known for growing high quality fruit and shrub root stock. According to Esther, her husband Clarke and George Rogers did most of the planting around Oswego's Catholic church.

Mary S. Young—for whom the West Linn Park is named—shopped frequently at Pilkington Nursery. Esther, who worked at the nursery, remembers the rumble of the pickup truck Mary drove whenever she came to the nursery. What a sight that must have been in the early 1900s—a woman behind the wheel—of a pickup, no less! She also remembered how Mary and Clarke tromped around the nursery together selecting plants, then worked like Trojans getting everything planted in a timely manner.

Speaking of planting in timely manner, Mary recalled a story about the landscape architects designing the stadium at Stanford University who ordered trees from the nursery. "They

Pilkington Nursery sign
UNIVERSITY OF OREGON LIBRARY

wanted them in February; it was planting time in California; but we couldn't ship because we were having a tremendous storm here with lots of snow and ice. The snow and ice was so heavy it broke the marquee over the Benson Hotel. But Stanford wanted their trees! They just couldn't understand why we had to delay shipping."

The original J.B. Pilkington Nursery began as a fruit tree farm owned by Pilkington's father, a practicing eye and ear doctor. In 1887, at only 16, John B. Pilkington, Jr., took over the farm and established an official nursery business. Fruit trees were in great demand and the nursery expanded rapidly.

Then the money panic hit in 1893, forcing Pilkington to close. He reopened in either 1896 or 1899 (some confusion about the date) on Columbia Boulevard in north Portland with a heavy emphasis on ornamental shrubs. When the Nursery outgrew its Columbia Boulevard location, John B. purchased 400 acres near Durham. The actual purchase consisted of two parcels of land; one located in Durham near the vicinity of what is now Bridgeport Village, and the other near what is now Pilkington Road.

In 1926, Pilkington, Jr., decided to open a branch nursery in Millbrae, California. Son Clarke ran the Durham operation, shipping many railroad cars loaded with trees to "Dad." John

B. Pilkington, Jr., although he followed in the footsteps of his father, did more than just expand the fruit tree farm business. He pioneered the importation of hundreds of varieties of trees and shrubs from Europe and Japan and was responsible for testing new plant varieties sent to him by U.S. government horticulturists.

"Dad"(John, Jr.) died in 1939. After his death, his wife Nellie sold much of the nursery; but Clarke and Esther kept the greenhouses and some of the land. They continued in the nursery business until 1955. Clarke became a well-known known master grafter and propagator. Nursery stock grown, grafted, and propagated by J.B. Pilkington Nursery was sold throughout the United States.

Clarke Pilkington died in 1969 at the age of 73. Esther moved from the house at 1615 SW Upper Boones Ferry to Raleigh Hills to be near her daughters, grandchildren, and great grandchildren. Esther was 96 when she passed away in 1989.

NOTE: John B. Pilkington built and owned a house at 1007 Lake Front Road in Lake Oswego. Like other houses around the lake at the time—and there weren't many—most were not primary dwellings. They were summer cottages. Pilkington intended to use the house during the summers, but never did. Wally and Helen Grigg purchased the house and lived in it until Helen's passing in 2013. Helen Grigg was a well-known educator, historian and founder of Oswego Quilters. The group met weekly and quilted in her home for over 50 years.

I Married a Taxidermist

Born Felicie Marie Virginie Puylaert (1889–1974)—later spelled Pollard—Lucy Pollard is considered one of Oswego's early pioneer women. The fourth of eight children, Lucy was only 3 months old when her family came to Oregon. The discovery of iron in Oswego motivated Lucy's father to move the family from Michigan to Oregon. Although he had worked in foundries in Michigan, Peter (Puylaert) Pollard was intrigued by the possibilities he'd heard about out west.

The family settled first in the Old Town area of Oswego in 1890. Pollard went to work at the Oswego smelter. However, after a 40-foot fall put a nasty gash in his head, Peter Pollard was forced to give up this risky kind of work, and Lucy's mother resolved that the family turn to farming and become self-sufficient.

The family moved from Old Town to a ten-acre farm on what is now Bergis Road. Across from Sacred Heart Cemetery, the property ran along a portion of Stafford Road next to the golf course and extended from both sides of Bergis Road down to McVey Avenue. Theresa Truchot remembers (*In Their Own Words*): "Lucy found and purchased the acreage. She loved that home and the gentle land. It had a well, fertile soil, and raised good crops. At harvest time the family would polish and scrub up the carrots, beets, and turnips; tie them into bundles; load them into the horse-drawn farm cart and ride through Oswego selling their produce."

Married life for Lucy was a bit unusual. She married taxidermist Edmond Gonty in late 1919, after a six-month courtship that, if not "arranged" by the Pollard and Gonty elders, was heavily influenced by their respective Belgian families. Gonty, like Lucy's parents Peter and Johanna, was born in Belgium. He came to Portland with his mother Mary and brother Edward in 1917, setting up a business on 2nd Avenue as a taxidermist. At that time Lucy was quite popular and had many options for marriage.

Lucy Pollard

Mary Gonty, a robust German woman, lived with the couple, but *never spoke* to Lucy. For two years Lucy suffered the silent treatment. She often told her mother how unhappy she was and, after her parents died, Lucy and Edmond divorced. She returned to the family farm and gentle land she loved, where she grew beets, turnips, carrots. Lucy owned a small home in Oswego, which she moved out to the farm property. She lived there until her death in 1974. It's not clear what happened to mother-in-law Mary. Lucy's ex-husband remarried widow Anna Jane Bewley in September 1931.

Educated in the first schools built in Oswego, Lucy developed a love of books. When she wasn't farming or reading, she visited Helen Grigg's quilting group. That group is still quilting—and has been for over 50 years. Throughout her life Lucy maintained an avid interest in the history of the area and local pioneer families. Nellie Kyle remembers that "Lucy used to attend the funeral services at Oswego Cemetery on Stafford Road so she could "visit with the old-timers."

*Lucy speaks**

Lucy Pollard is my name
Farming is my game.

I was born in 1889, the 20th of December;
84 years later, my death, the sixth month after September.
(March 1974)

My family were early settlers here,
1890 was the year.
We lived on a farm off what is now Bergis Road.
Carrots, beets, turnips are what we sowed.

Oswego Pioneer Cemetery was just across the way.
Quirky, I know, but I visited almost every day.
My father built the Catholic church at 1st & E;
The family walked 2 ½ miles to Mass,
Mom carrying me.

I married Ed Gonty, a taxidermist.
His mother I longed to smack with my fist.
She was a robust German bloke.
Neither of us to the other ever spoke.

After 2 years of silence Ed & I said our goodbyes,
Regrets I had none and uttered nary a sigh.

Great loves of mine,
Gardening
And books of any kind.

*CHANNELED BY THE AUTHOR

Postmistresses and Postmaster

Charlotte Calkins served as Oswego's first female postmaster in 1863 followed by Mrs. Lucy E. Prosser, wife of grocery owner George Prosser, in 1876. However, Wesley Hull was Oswego's very first postmaster when the post office was established on December 31, 1854, before Oregon was granted statehood. Often the post office was located in the home or business of the current postmaster and such was the case with George Prosser, who served as postmaster after Lucy, in 1888. During George's time of service, the post office was located in his grocery on Durham Street in a little white house right next to the Peg Tree. The house was known as Cottage Hill.

The first rural mail route started in 1905 with Jess Coon delivering mail in a two-wheeled horse-drawn cart. Lester Clinefelter took over the reins in 1910, delivering the mail on horseback. Clifford "Happy" Johnson, who followed Clinefelter in 1912, delivered mail in a white delivery wagon pulled by a team of horses. His first day on the job Johnson's horses spooked and kicked the $90 vehicle to pieces. It had to be rebuilt, but was never the same. His next delivery vehicle was an automobile—a Ford, of course. Roads were not maintained in those days, which meant Johnson had to carry some sort of chopping device with him so he could clear brush and branches out of the way to get the car through.

Letters in the early days were addressed simply "John Smith Oswego, O.T." (Oregon Territory). The postmaster would buy an ad in the *Oregon Spectator* newspaper—the area's first local paper based in Oregon City—letting people know that mail was available for pick up. When residents picked up their mail, they paid the postmaster for the ad. Many of Oswego's postmasters are buried in Oswego Pioneer Cemetery: Lucy and George Prosser, Cliff Johnson, Jess Coon, Lucien Davidson, Ben Lombardo.

By the 1950s, the post office was located at the Oswego Country Store on 2nd Street between A and B Avenues. Rapid growth forced the post office to move again into what used be Oswego Auto Parts on B street just off State. The final location of the post office came in 1959 with the completion of a new building at 4th & B, where it is today.

Oswego's first mail carrier, Jess Coon

Mary Got the Mines... Did Henry Get the Shaft?

Henry and Mary Prosser left Iowa in 1852 with their three children to come to Oregon, wintering at old Fort Hall until the following spring. They arrived in Oregon on June 25, 1853, and immediately filed for a donation land claim of 300 acres that ran the length of Oswego Lake Golf Course, east along Country Club Road, south and west along Iron Mountain Road, and north into the hills above Lake Oswego Hunt Club.

As stipulated by the government in the Donation Land Claim Act, recipients were required to make the land productive within five years in exchange for not having to pay for it. Henry and Mary Prosser built a house and farmed their land claim.

For whatever reason, Henry left the farm—and his wife and son—and disappeared. Mary, at the urging of son George, attempted to file for divorce, but the court blamed Mary for her husband's abandonment and wouldn't grant the divorce. The court changed its mind, however, granting her the divorce and sole title to the Prosser donation land claim when Frances Tryon (Socrates Tryon's widow) and others testified on her behalf. The land claim eventually became the "Prosser Mine." One hundred-fifty-five acres became Oswego Lake Country Club and Golf Course in 1924.

Ore was discovered here in 1861 and first mined from the Patton mine located just north of Oswego Creek in New Town (now First Addition). Who discovered the ore on the Prosser land claim is unclear, but Oregon Iron and Steel heard there was ore "in them thar hills" and wanted to get their hands on it. Mary Prosser leased the ore bed (i.e., iron mine) to Oregon Iron and Steel in 1867.

She sold the Prosser property and the mines in 1873 to Hawley, Dodd and Company—a group of Portland investors who were acting as agents of the Oregon Iron Company. In addition to the sale of the mines, Mary earned income operating a boarding house in town for the workers employed by Oregon Iron and Steel. Although she was a successful pioneer businesswoman, Mary Prosser could not read or write. When her signature was required, she signed with an "X." George aided his mother in the handling of her business transactions. Mary Prosser died in 1873, leaving George to commence business on his own.

George Prosser, son of Mary and Henry Prosser

George W. Prosser owned the Durham block in Old Town— the area south and east of Lakewood Center including George Rogers Park, between the Grange Hall and Church Street. He built and opened Processor's Grocery on Durham Street, very close to the Odd Fellows Hall, using bricks and lumber salvaged after a fire burned the original Albert A. Durham house. In 1896, Furnace Street became the preferred residential area for many prominent families. Prosser built a new family home there and moved his store from Old Town to New Town (now First Addition).

Because general stores were often places where townsfolk gathered, they became local drop-off points for mail. Prosser's Store served as a post office and George served as one of the original postmasters. Robberies in the early days were not uncommon but what was uncommon about the robbery of Prosser's Store and post office in 1909 was the letter he received from the burglar telling him how much he enjoyed spending the money he stole. "I have just drunk your health in a bottle of Mum's Extra Dry, at $7.50" (nearly $200 today).

A memoir about the Prossers written by Esther Watson states that George, wife Susie, and daughters Sylver and Dena used to bicycle some 60 miles from Portland up to Government Camp. At the Toll Gate they had to push their bicycles uphill the last 10 miles.

George Prosser was always the first man of the season to travel the Mt. Hood Road (now Highway 26) after the winter break. Susie accompanied him, but was not recognized as the "first woman of the season to travel the road." She was praised, however, in an article in *The Oregonian* (May 9, 1900): "the achievement of Mrs. Prosser is one a man might as well cherish as an athletic performance."

Travelling the Mt. Hood Road in the 1900s by car, by wagon, on horseback or bicycle, was arduous, uncomfortable, tiring and trying, and often resulted in passengers becoming caked with mud or dust, depending on the season. It definitely required athletic ability.

A very interesting and informative book about the history of Government Camp and the Mt. Hood Road, written by Ivan M. Wooley, is titled *Off to Mt. Hood*. The book, published by the Oregon Historical Society, is still in print and available at libraries.

Considered a pillar of the community, George Prosser was a member of the Odd Fellows. Their mission was to take care of families of those who had passed away. George personally arranged burials for many families and attended the services when he could. His strong interest in helping with burials possibly stemmed from George's loss of his three daughters before the age of three. George and his father-in-law Jesse Bullock donated part of the Bullock donation land claim for Oswego Pioneer Cemetery and neighboring Sacred Heart Cemetery.

In 1880, George Prosser was elected to the Oregon Legislature on the Republican ticket, serving two years. He became superintendent of Oswego School District, No. 47. George was always ready and willing to promote the interests of the county and town he lived in, except when there was a movement afoot to incorporate Oswego. He was adamantly opposed to the idea, but eventually changed his mind.

George's first wife, Lucy Bullock—daughter of Nancy and Jesse Bullock—became Oswego's first post mistress—before George did. Lucy and George married sometime between 1871 and 1873. She passed away in 1887 at the age of 36. George married his second wife Gerhardina (Dena) Brownleewe in 1888. Dena and George had three children: Sylver, born in 1890; George T. in 1891; daughter Dena in 1893. Susan became George's third wife in 1896. George died in 1917 at 80. He, along with his mother and his children, are buried at Oswego Pioneer Cemetery.

The lease agreement is on display at the historic Worker's Cottage in Lake Oswego, as part of the Lake Oswego Preservation Society collection.

To Market, to Market

LOCATED AT Bryant Road and Lower Drive, in the building where Deno's Pizza and Aji-Tram (previously 7-Eleven) are now located, Chet Remsen and his wife Evelyn bought Emmons Grocery in 1947, renaming it Remsen's Market and Grocery. A family-managed, community-minded business, Remsen's was a popular place to shop for groceries because of their high-quality meats and produce and the family friendly atmosphere.

Jim Rathbun, a classmate, neighbor and history buff, wrote me after this article ran in my November 2017 column: "Dunis... once again you've walked me down memory lane. When my parents were first married in 1948 and living over by the lake off South Shore, my Mom shopped at Remsen's Market, the old store. She loved that place and shopped there until Wizer's became the dominant food store at the other end of town (which worked better since we were then living in the big house on Iron Mountain Blvd.)."

When Chet and Evelyn began to feel "a bursting at the seams," they decided to enlarge and remodel the old market on adjoining property. Because the adjoining property was situated on a steep hill, architects advised that the new store and the old store should be connected, so the old building could be used for storage and backroom operations. The remodel began in 1959 and was completed about 6 months later in 1960, according to Chet Remsen's son, Bill. The new store was renamed Remsen's Lakeside Thriftway. Chet Remsen retired in 1967, selling his pride and joy to the McKays Grocery chain. McKays sustained a terrible fire not long after it opened and the building remained vacant until a new tenant took it over.

For the 1959 remodel, Chet consulted with Elmo McKeel of Portland's Elmo McKeel Company, a leader in grocery store design, construction, installation, and equipment supply, to assist with building the new store. As soon as a design was agreed upon, Elmo and his staff went to work installing a bank of water-cooled compressors, laying new refrigeration lines, and removing the old meat lockers. The old "locker room" was completely remodeled into a large, refrigerated cutting room with freezer space.

Lighting for the store was engineered by Sam Sposito of Lighting Specialties, also located in Portland. In an article in *Oregon Independent Grocer* Sam is quoted, "The lighting was designed with the shopper in mind, having the distribution of the light at the point of sale. For example, the produce section would have the minimum amount of light."

Remsen's Thriftway, according to another *Oregon Independent Grocer* magazine article, was a completely Hussman-McKeel-equipped market. Everything—from self-service refrigeration cases, to shelving, to state-of-the-art check stands—was custom built in Hussman-McKeel's own factory. The check stands, known as Fast-Flo, were designed and built to look beautiful, handle large orders quickly in a small space, and prevent checker fatigue.

Some of the folks who worked at Remsen's besides owners Chet and Evelyn Remsen and their sons Bill and Jim: In the produce department was Bill Pendergrass, who couldn't keep the mouth-watering displays replenished fast enough, because they could be seen from almost any point in the store. Leonard Lumby, the butcher, claimed he couldn't cut meat fast enough to satisfy customer demand. Operating the new in-store bakery were Mr. and Mrs. Gus Miro, well known in the bakery trade.

Remsen's Thriftway packed a lot of punch into 6,000 square feet of space. In addition to the Hussman-McKeel fixtures, probably the most unique feature of the store was not the amount of selling space, but the family living quarters situated directly above the grocery in the same building. "The upstairs living quarters were always part of the old store and never changed when the store was remodeled. They are today as they were then," comments Remsen, "but have been converted into business offices."

One more bit from Jim Rathbun: "My first job in the grocery business (as a senior at Lake Oswego High School) was at the Remsen's new store that burned down after the Remsens sold it. (The guys who bought it from the Remsens weren't doing very well with it and, low and behold, a 'mysterious' fire occurred in the middle of the night (starting in the back room). Better yet, the fire department showed up to extinguish that blaze and ran their hoses from a hydrant up the hill—from that hydrant the hoses had to cross the train tracks and shortly after the hoses started shooting water into the blaze, the nightly train came through on schedule and severed the fire hoses—so much for that water source to fight the fire with. When it was finally put out, the store was gutted, although still standing, and the new owners faded into the sunset shortly thereafter. I moved on to work at Safeway in Lake Oswego (Spring, 1967) which was a great job that kept me in cash through most of college. For me, it all started with Mr. and Mrs Remsen, who were wonderful people."

Thanks for the story ... a classic, for sure!

A Talented Presswoman

FAMILY, FRIENDS, WRITERS and journalists would agree. The award-winning Elizabeth Salway Ryan earned a living as the news editor for the *Lake Oswego Review* for 22 years, from 1946 to 1968. Her Lake Oswego legacy is considerable.

The Beth Ryan Collection of 700 photographs she took during her tenure as a journalist is archived at the Lake Oswego Library; the collection can be accessed online anytime. Cliff Newell wrote in a *Review* article in 2010, "The collection came about serendipitously. The library already had many of her photos, but not enough to warrant calling it a full-fledged collection."

Ryan's granddaughter Lois Moll changed that when she went to a photo-scanning event at the library. After her grandmother passed away, Moll lived in Ryan's house in the Sunny Hill area. Moll says she's spent years and years sorting through everything in the basement, wondering what to do with all of "gramma's" photographs. "After I attended that scanning event, I knew the library was the place for them," she recollects.

After Moll made the first contribution of Ryan's photos to the library, the collection continued to grow as Shirley and Bob Kronquist—Ryan's daughter and son-in-law—also donated photos to be scanned. Library volunteer Pat Snider, who assisted with creating the Ryan collection, remembers Ryan's large "horn-rimmed glasses with the rhinestones" and all the photos of pancakes she took over the years at the 4th of July Lions Club Pancake Breakfast.

In addition to the Beth Ryan Collection of photographs, Lake Oswego honored the legendary journalist by naming a park after her, the Beth Ryan Nature Preserve. Ryan, an avid gardener, advocated adamantly for protecting open spaces long before it became popular.

Beth Ryan at her desk wearing her "winged rhinestone glasses"

Ryan's journalistic accomplishments are numerous. The most prestigious achievement came in 1971 when she was the runner-up for the Woman of Achievement Award given by the National Federation of Press Women in 1970. In 1971, she was given the Off-Beat Award by The Portland Professional Chapter of Theta Sigma (now Women in Communication). Ryan won three first place awards in 1953 from the Oregon Presswomen:

best news story in a weekly paper; best feature story in a magazine, and best column in a weekly. As a result of a family history course Ryan taught at Clackamas Community College, she compiled and edited an anthology of writing by her students, *Leaves From Family Trees*. The anthology was published in 1978.

Born in 1910, Elizabeth Salway graduated from Franklin High School in 1923 and from the University of Oregon in 1931 with a journalism degree. She married Cornelius Ryan in 1932, whom she later divorced. After the divorce, she moved in 1938 with her father and three young children to Sunny Hill Farm located near Oswego Pioneer Cemetery. As her obituary in the *Lake Oswego Review* stated: "During her time on the farm, she wrote radio scripts and poems about current events while also pitching hay, canning food, and milking cows. During WWII she was the women's editor of the *Oregon City Enterprise,* offering hints on how to cope with wartime shortages." In those early days, Ryan would often ride her horse to gather stories.

Ryan's last column before moving to Taipei, China, in 1968 to became editor of *The China Post* appeared in the *Review* October 10, 1968. She wrote, "Taiwan is a beautiful island, so I'm hoping some of you will come see it—and me. And in two years, I hope to return to my now-cleaned-off desk at the *Review.* Aloha." The legendary, award-winning writer passed away in 1995 at 85.

The House that John Built

"I MET JOHN C. TRULLINGER. Well, not exactly," wrote Lake Oswego resident Henry Germond in an article for the Oswego Heritage House and Museum's newsletter in 2012. "I was dining in a restaurant in Astoria and they had a book on display by local author Bryan Penttila, titled *Columbia River: The Astoria Odyssey,* published by Frank Amato Publications of Portland, Oregon, in 2003. I perused through the book...

"Pentilla wrote of Trullinger, *'This wildly successful entrepreneur had tried his hand at everything from panning gold to processing wheat to producing pig iron before settling in Astoria to oversee the construction and management of his sawmill in the late 1870s.'"*

Trullinger plats Oswego

Although Albert Alonzo Durham named Oswego, laid out the original town site, and is considered the father of Oswego, he never officially filed the plat documents. John Corse Trullinger did, in 1867. He filed the official plat with street names honoring many of those associated with Oregon Iron and Steel (see "Who's in a Name," p. 172). Trullinger marked blocks one and two using the first casting of pig iron from the furnace. The pig iron at Ladd and Durham streets is still in place. Interesting to note that there is no street named Trullinger... but there should be.

John Corse Trullinger patented seven machines including a triple turbine water wheel that was much more efficient than

John Trullinger and Hannah Boyles Trullinger
ACCESSGENEALOGY.COM

the water wheels in use at the time. Seeking opportunities to profit from his invention, Trullinger saw a golden nugget when Durham's turbine water wheel became outdated in 1860—ten years after it was installed. He purchased Durham's sawmill; made improvements including the turbine; and renamed the mill Oswego Milling Company. Oswego Milling Company's primary product was sidewalk lumber for Portland streets.

Transporting finished lumber from his mill, as well as produce, people, and other goods from around the area, to Portland was a challenge, as was getting goods (including timber) from the Tualatin Valley to the mill. Together with the Sucker Lake and Tualatin River Railroad and the People's Transportation Company, John Trullinger plotted a new route between Portland and the Tualatin Valley that avoided portaging around Willamette Falls and would mean less expense getting logs from the Tualatin Valley to Oswego Milling Company.

Wheat, logs, and travelers to Portland went downriver aboard the steamer *Onward*, then took the Sucker Lake and Tualatin River Railroad to Colfax Landing, and steamed over Sucker Lake (Oswego Lake) aboard the *Minnehaha*, built by Trullinger's Oswego Milling Company.

Heavily investing in the transportation industry—a railway and boats for moving goods to market—Trullinger saw as one of the surest ways to make a fortune on the Oregon frontier. However, this didn't pan out, and Trullinger sold the town site and sawmill sometime after 1870.

The Move to Astoria

In 1853, John Corse Trullinger married Hannah Boyles. According to an article in *The Oregonian* written in 1867, "Mrs. J.C. Trullinger has a fine and costly dwelling nearly completed on the corner of Ladd and Durham Streets." The house was moved twice and eventually demolished in the 1990s. Boyles was not only Trullinger's life partner, but also his business mentor, and shared in much of Trullinger's successes.

After the sale of the Oswego Milling Company, in the late 1870s the Trullingers moved to Astoria, where Trullinger built a bigger sawmill with more technological advances than the Oswego mill. A fire leveled Astoria in 1883, but Trullinger was lucky. His sawmill was the only one remaining. Most of Astoria was rebuilt using lumber from his mill. By 1885 the mill was generating electricity by burning wood waste to make steam that lit many of the newly constructed buildings in Astoria.

Having an interest in politics, Trullinger served a term in the state legislature and also served as mayor-elect of Astoria for two years.

John Corse Trullinger was born July 29, 1829, in Fountain Cty, Indiana, and arrived in Oregon in 1848 from Iowa. He died April 28, 1908, in Astoria.

Durham's vision for Oswego: Develop a sawmill town; Trullinger's vision: Transform the struggling sawmill town into a thriving manufacturing town. Neither of these visions materialized. Interesting to note that both Durham and Trullinger left Oswego: Durham moved west toward Tualatin (Durham Road area is named for him) and Trullinger moved to Astoria. Neither of them is buried at Oswego Pioneer Cemetery.

Art Under Cover Uncovered

It's back! The mosaic mural created in 1964 for the Safeway at 5th & A by Arvid Orbeck with the help of his wife Shirley has been uncovered. Arvid Orbeck was born and educated in Oslo, Norway. He graduated from the Royal School of Arts and Crafts with a diploma in graphic design and also received a Fulbright Scholarship to Parsons School of Design in New York. Friendships made at that school brought him to Portland. In Portland, Arvid and Shirley, also a designer, started Orbeck Design. Orbeck fulfilled a two-year contract—the largest ever given for major art projects since the 1930s—for the Army Corps of Engineers and Lake Oswego Safeway.

Installed when the store was built in 1963, the Safeway mosaic mural is a map of Lake Oswego. It contains many symbols of the town including the lake, the Country Club, and Lake Oswego Hunt. Arvid and Shirley created the swirling rock pattern surrounding the mural's tiled area on their hands and knees pushing river rocks into the sand. After they finished, they felt it looked better "upside down." The rest of the mural was made by creating a form flat on the ground with a bed of leveled sand. The rocks you

Arvid Orbeck

see on Safeway's walls were individually set by experienced stone masons. Then slurry and concrete were poured. When all was cured, the wall was raised vertically into position, revealing the rock.

Originally, the mosaic mural was on an outside wall on the southeast corner of the building, but as a result of a remodel in the 1990s, it was enclosed inside the store. Another remodel in 2003 completely covered the mural with a wall of sheetrock. Now, however, the mosaic wall has been brought back into view where it can once again be admired, enjoyed, and appreciated by the community. The mural is now part of a supporting wall in the floral department, so it cannot be removed.

Shirley Orbeck (center) gazes at the wall behind which their mosaic mural was covered over and then uncovered. At left is Corinna Campbell-Sak.

The Safeway mural was the precursor of major wall sculptures, displays, tile murals, signage, and wall graphics Arvid created for The Dalles and John Day dams, the sculpted concrete walls of Chemeketa Community College, and wood sculpture walls for the U.S. Bank building, Orbeck's artistic range was extensive, moving beyond the design of printed matter such as books and magazines, to graphic identification for businesses. Portland State University, Kah/Nee/Ta Vacation Resort, Mt. Bachelor Ski Area plus a few local businesses; Mountain Park, Red Fox

Hills, and the Bay Roc were all among his clients. He was also known for his innovative furniture designs commissioned for *Family Circle, House Beautiful,* and *Better Homes & Gardens.* And he created a series of limited edition serigraphs for the Matson Lines.

Arvid Orbeck was one of the most influential designers in the Pacific Northwest. Orbeck Design received National and International awards from the Advertising Club of New York. He had exhibitions at the Portland Art Museum, Portland State University, and the Museum of Modern Art in Norway. Orbeck taught Graphic Design as Lecturer in Art at Portland State University for 13 years. He served on the Governor's Advisory Committee for the Arts in Oregon, was advisor to the Metropolitan Arts Commission Gallery Committee in Portland, and served on the arts advisory commission in Lake Oswego.

Arvid Orbeck passed away in 1988.

Birdwatching in the Northwest

WHEN I FIRST encountered the name Twining, I thought it was the Twinings of tea fame. Fame, yes; but not tea.

Frances Staver and Charles Twining were born and raised in Monroe, Winconsin. They married in 1909, heading west to Oregon four years later in 1913. Before they married, Charles enjoyed a career as a bank president. Frances studied at Northwestern University Prep School for two years in the College of Liberal Arts followed by an interval of travel. She graduated in 1899 from the University of Wisconsin with honors in English and a B.L. degree—Bachelor of Law. Immediately after Frances said "I do," she became the stepmother to Charles' eight children.

Upon their arrival in Oregon, the Twinings settled in the Glenmorrie area on top of the hill in what is now Skylands. About 1917 they designed and built an elegant home down near the Willamette River. There were only four families living in the area at the time: Twinings, Shepherds, Owens, and Moreys.

Frances Staver Twining loved gardening, birds, and books. She and Charles inherited the vast library belonging to Great Grandpa Twining, claiming a first edition of Washington Irving, a complete set of first editions by John Burroughs, and some lovely editions of John Muir's books.

Brothers Clarence and Ed Twining said "It Was All About the Birds"

Clarence Twining recollects: "Our stepmother Frances first got interested in birds because they were around everywhere.

They'd come right up and sit on the windowsill like pets. That started it. She began studying them, making lots and lots of notes." Her note-taking led to jobs first at *The Oregon Journal*, then *The Oregonian*.

Frances Twining also contributed to other well-known publications such as *Sunset, Christian Science Monitor, American Home,* and *Horticulture.* She served as Associate Editor for *Better Flowers* and its successor *Western Homes and Gardens* for two years. In addition to writing, Frances served as the national president of the Alpha Phi Fraternity. She belonged to the American Association of University Women and to the National Society of New England Women.

> *"I have tried to put into words how wonderful a thing it is for an everyday person like myself to win the companionship of birds."*
>
> *Frances Stover Twining*

Although her articles featured gardening ideas, tips, etc., Frances always included something about birds. The two seemed to go hand in hand, so she kept observing birds and taking notes. "Mostly her interest centered around the songbirds," remembers stepson Ed Twining. " I thought they would carry our place away. We had rafts of birdhouses and birdbaths and that sort of stuff. Mom was always feeding them while I was knocking off the pheasants with a shotgun.

"Dad liked gardening, too, and landscaping. He used to dig up all manner of trees and shrubs from what we called a 'park' Mr. Morey built. Dad would move 'his findings' from Morey's abandoned garden to our place, much to my dismay. When he found a tree or shrub he recognized, he would sell them."

Frances writes *Birdwatching in the West*

Peter Binford, of Binford and Mort Publishing (a.k.a. Binfords & Mort Publishing and Metropolitan Printing Co.) asked Frances to write a book about birds. She told her husband, "I shouldn't write that book because I'm not an expert on birds." He replied, "Well maybe that's a good thing, because now you will do a lot of research and will write a very good book." And that's what she did. The book is titled *Bird Watching in the West*.

Something I discovered about Frances Twining: she also had an interest in people with disabilities. In 1926 Frances wrote an article about John Auer, a blind man who made violins, for the *Journal of Visual Impairment and Blindness*.

Frances Twining's book — cover and endsheet spread
AUTHOR'S COPY

Chairman Joint Chiefs of Staff

"I DREAMED of becoming a naval officer, but test anxiety got the best of me. I failed the Naval Academy entrance exam and attended West Point instead, from 1917–1918, graduating as a Second Lieutenant of Infantry in 1918."

General Nathan F. Twining (1857–1982) served in the Army infantry for three years, then was reassigned to the Air Service Corps where he flew fighter aircrafts for 15 years and was a flight instructor. At the same time, he attended the Air Corps Tactical School and the Command and General Staff College.

General Nathan Twining, Chairman Joint Chiefs of Staff
OFFICE OF THE JOINT CHIEFS OF STAFF

Twining became chief of staff of the Allied air forces in the South Pacific in 1942. The following year he was promoted to Brigadier General, assuming command of the Thirteenth Air Force and the Fifteenth Air Force shortly thereafter. On one of Major General Twining's missions in 1943 from Guadalcanal to Espiritu Santo in the New Hebrides, he was forced to ditch his plane. He and 14 others survived six days in a life raft until the Navy rescued them.

Brig. Gen. Twining also commanded the Twentieth Air Force, leading three B-29s in developing a new route from Guam to Washington via India and Germany. They completed the 13,167-mile trip in 59 hours, 30 minutes.

At some point during his career (educated guess is around 1930s, but not able to confirm this), General Twining married Maude McKeever of Oahu, Hawaii. They had three children: Captain Robert G., Nathan A., and Olivia B.

When Brigadier General Twining returned to the States, he was named head of the Air Material Command, taking over the Alaskan Air Command in 1947. After three years at the Alaskan Air Command, Lieutenant General Twining planned to retire. However, Twining became the Vice Chief of Staff of the U.S. Air Force and received a promotion to full general when Muir Fairchild, previous Chief of Staff of the Air Force, died of a heart attack unexpectedly.

General Twining become Chief of Staff of the United States Air Force in 1953. This was followed in 1957 with his appointment to Chairman of the Joint Chiefs of Staff by President Eisenhower. General Twining became the first Air Force officer to serve as Chairman of the Joint Chiefs of Staff.

President Eisenhower (center) swearing in General Nathan Twining

Eisenhower re-appointed Twining Chairman for a second term in 1959; but he elected to take early retirement from active duty in 1960 due to deteriorating health conditions resulting from major surgery.

Following his retirement, Twining worked as vice chairman for the publishing firm Holt, Rinehart and Winston. General Twining received the General William E. Mitchell Memorial Award in 1965. This is just one of 33 awards, decorations, and honors General Twining received during his lifetime.

He died March 28, 1982, at age 85, at Lackland Air Force Base in Texas, and is buried at Arlington National Cemetery. His wife, Maude M. Twining, is buried alongside him.

Wallings Leave a Legacy of Fruit and Education

GEORGE AND FRANCIS Walling left a major legacy in the Lake Oswego area: Part of their donation land claim became the site of The Christie School for Girls on the Marylhurst College campus and the old Walling home served as a dormitory for students for many years.

George Washington Walling was born December 18, 1818, in Ohio, and moved with his parents, Lucy and Gabriel Walling, to Iowa in 1828. Restless, the senior Wallings and their son George, his wife Francis, and other members of the family headed west in 1847.

The Wallings settled in Oregon City. They lived there for two years while seeking a donation land claim. George found work as a shipbuilder. In 1849, he and his wife selected a 640-acre property on the west bank of the Willamette River, a short distance upstream from Sucker (Oswego) Creek and adjacent to the land claim of his parents.

Residing on the land claim were George and Francis, their children Albert and Adam, 11 single men, several farmers and carpenters, and George's brother Albert. (The senior Albert later became one of Oregon's most prominent printers and publishers in the 1880s. He established the printing house of A.G. Walling, where he published the *Oregon Farmer* and the *North Pacific Rural Spirit*.)

George established Willamette Nursery on his farm and operated it for nearly 40 years before he turned it over to his sons. He was well known for the quality of his fruit trees and ornamental shrubs, and was one of the early developers of the Major Francis cherry and the Champion prune.

In addition to being a nurseryman, George Walling served for more than 15 years as Clackamas County Superintendent of Schools. His sons Albert and Adam were longtime residents of Oswego. Albert took over the operation of Willamette Nursery in the 1880s, changing the name to Oswego Nursery and running the operation for 25 years. George died on June 10, 1891.

Other farmers in the area specializing in fruit orchards were Henderson Luelling and John B. Pilkington (see p. 121). Luelling, considered the father of the Pacific Northwest fruit industry, brought 1,000 grafted fruit trees in two wagons filled with soil, manure, and charcoal across

Transport used by George Walling at his nursery to haul picked fruit. Walling developed the Major Francis cherry and the Champion prune.

the Oregon Trail. In spite of expert agricultural advice that he would never make it, Henderson, his family, and 800 of the original grafted fruit trees survived the journey to Oregon. Upon his arrival here in 1848, Henderson Luelling established an orchard in Milwaukie at the mouth of Johnson Creek, now the site of Waverly Country Club. Many of Luelling's fruit trees became the parent stock of most of the orchards in Oregon's Willamette Valley.

Henderson's brother, Seth Luelling, and head orchardist Ah Bing developed and grafted the ever popular Bing cherry in 1875.

Marylhurst campus was constructed on the donation land claims of Jesse Bullock and George Walling.

MARYLHURST.EDU

A Brief History of Marylhurst

Founded by an order of nuns from Quebec, Canada, in 1859, 12 sisters of the Holy Names of Jesus and Mary arrived in Portland and within two weeks established St. Mary's Academy for Girls downtown. The Sisters purchased land overlooking the Willamette River in 1906 from Jesse Bullock and George Walling, who each held a donation land claim on the property at the time. This was also the site of the Jaresche family farm. The sisters christened the land purchase "Villa Maria."

The Provincial House was constructed on the Villa Maria site in 1911 to serve as headquarters for the Oregon Province of the Holy Names of Jesus and Mary. The Sisters renamed the Villa Maria site Marylhurst, creating the new name from Mary, mother of Jesus, and hurst, meaning woods. The Sisters added an 'l' between Mary and hurst to give it a better sound. They felt the name Marylhurst was more apropos to the location of property and lent itself better to their vision of an extended educational campus.

FOURTH STOP
On the Water

Ladd Estate Company brochure advertising homes
for sale in the Lake Oswego Country Club District

OREGON HISTORICAL SOCIETY

—Slogan created by Paul C. Murphy,
President, Ladd Estate Company

Lake Grove Swim Park

"RIDE THE RED ELECTRIC from Portland to Oswego's free picnic grounds at Lake View Park (west end of Oswego Lake)" read the brochure promoting the sale of homes in the Lake View Villas area, the first platted subdivision in Oswego. The homes were sited at the north and west end of the lake and along the lakeshore below McVey Avenue.

Oregon Iron and Steel (OIS) owned a great deal of land around the lake. Facing rising debts, they decided to develop and sell off much of the property, using the lake as a draw to generate sales. Referred to as Lake View Villas, this was the first OIS venture away from the business of smelting iron and into residential real estate.

Since OIS owned the land, they developed Lake View Park as an outdoor sales office in 1913. Because of its close proximity to two Red Electric stops and to the Lake View Villas subdivision, they hoped to entice potential homebuyers by taking them on scenic tours around the lake by boat. OIS purchased *The Lotus,* a small launch with a colorful striped awning, which would meet passengers at the Lake Grove and Lake View Park Red Electric stations. Stops at the park always allowed time for refreshments, a swim, chit chat, and hopefully a home sale or two.

The Ladd Estate Company, under the auspices of Paul C. Murphy, managed OIS real estate investments. Since sales of Lake View Villas struggled, and the scenic tours marketing idea didn't prove cost effective, OIS and Ladd Estate decided to build a second, smaller and less costly sales office near Graef Circle

*Girls riding in gondola in front of Lake Grove Swim Park, 1920.
The gondola eventually sank in the lake.*

LOPL DIGITAL HISTORY COLLECTION: PHOTO DONATED BY PAUL F. MURPHY,
SON OF WELL-KNOWN LAKE OSWEGO REAL ESTATE DEVELOPER PAUL C. MURPHY.

close to Lake View Park at the intersection of South Shore and Lakeview Boulevard. (Graef Circle still exists today.) OIS offered Lake View Park to the Lake Grove Community. Twice they turned it down. Paul C. Murphy donated the park to the school board. Renamed Lake Grove Swim Park, it has been and still is operated by the Lake Oswego School District, serving residents living in the Lake Grove area.

Willa Wows 'em on Water

WATERSKI SHOWS as entertainment date back to the 1920s. Dick Pope, Sr., along with his wife Julie, converted part of a swamp on the shores of Lake Eloise into the well-known Cypress Gardens theme park in Winter Haven, Florida, in 1936. Pope was a flamboyant character often attired in a pink-trimmed turquoise suit, wearing bright white shoes.

Prior to Pope, the lesser-known Ralph Samuelson, inventor of waterskiing, made a name for himself performing tricks at summer water carnivals around Minnesota. At an exhibition on July 8, 1925, he performed the first ski jump on water. *Splat!* His first attempt didn't go well, but he landed the second one after greasing the platform surface with lard.

Samuelson, 22, made the world's first pair of skis out of pine planks, 8 feet long by 9 inches wide. He strapped these to his feet with bindings made from leather scraps he bought at a harness shop. The first tow rope was a 100-foot-long window sash cord Samuelson purchased from a hardware store. He talked a blacksmith into making an iron ring for a handle and his sister into painting the skis white. Across Lake Pepin, near Lake City, Minnesota, at age 22, he skimmed across the water. Many years later the American Waterski Association credited him with inventing the sport.

Following Samuelson and Pope, Lake Oswego's own Willa Worthington entered the scene in the '40s. "She could scramble eggs on water skis, never mixing the whites with the yolks," wrote *The Oregonian* (1947) about Willa's waterskiing

Willa Worthington poses with one of competitive trophies she won.
THE WESTERN WATERSKI MUSEUM

talents. Worthington, a blue-eyed blonde, started skiing at 14. "I was afraid to leave the dock because I thought I would split in half," Worthington told *The Oregonian*. "But after I got the feel of it I knew it was my sport." Worthington started skiing competitively at 16, earning 18 national titles. Pope, Sr., was enchanted with Willa and recruited her to perform with his Aquamaids show team at Cypress Gardens.

Not only was Worthington a star at Cypress Gardens, she played the role of Esther Williams in two movies, was the first to master the backward swan on skis and the first to ski over a jump backwards. (Sorry, Ralph.) Lynn Novakofski, Cypress Gardens show director, developed freestyle jumping, the four-tier pyramid and strap doubles moves, plus other innovations. His experience and interest in ice-skating and dance inspired him to refine doubles and the swivel. Many of the ballet moves Willa created are still being performed today by show teams such as Portland Water Spectacular.

Worthington introduced water ballet to Lake Oswego. She designed and made all the costumes—mostly out of shower curtains—for the first Lake Oswego Water Ski Festival held in September 1955 at George Rogers Park (formerly Oswego City Park).

Mrs. Wendell Schollander, mother of five-time Olympic gold medalist in swimming Don Schollander, followed Willa's lead, continuing to organize and promote water ballet in Oswego.

Festival organizers decided there should be a Grand Marshall for this inaugural event. Since "Neptune" was the prefix for Oswego phone numbers at the time, George Rogers was crowned "King Neptune" by popular vote. The Lake Oswego Water Festival continued for five years.

The second annual Lake Oswego Water Ski Festival in 1956 began at 8 P.M. with explosives signaling the first nighttime waterski show. The 1957 Oswego Water Ski Festival featured the Spencer family: Sharon, Bill, Diane and her husband Don Nichols. The fourth annual Lake Oswego Water Festival featured kite skiing and barefoot skiing. The Lake Oswego Water Ski Festival changed its name to Lake Oswego Ski Follies in 1959 and also changed its venue from the Willamette River to the 7,000-seat Oregon Centennial Aqua Center. (The author has no recollection of this venue.)

After retiring from competition in 1959, Willa Worthington McGuire Cook continued to waterski passionately for fun. She also supported the sport any way she could. The Grand Dame of waterskiing passed away April 21, 2017. She was 89.

Author Dunis and Frank LeSage, one of the few original PTers still living who worked to restore PT 658.
AUTHOR'S COLLECTION

Never Tell an Ex–PT Boater It Can't Be Done

PT STANDS FOR PATROL TORPEDO. The only PT boat in the world that is operational, thanks to a dedicated group of WWII volunteer vets, is housed at the Swan Island Coast Guard and Naval Reserve Center in Portland.

Built at Higgins Industries Boatworks in New Orleans in 1945, PT 658 was originally slated to be part of Squadron 45, but was never placed into commission. Instead it was destined for Russia, but when the war ended, the shipment was halted and PT 658 was assigned to the Bureau of Aeronautics as a "remote control target" at Naval Air Facility, Pt. Mugu, California. PT 658 was reclassified again Dec. 3, 1948, as "Floating Equipment."

Ten years later (June 30, 1958), the U.S. Navy sold PT 658 as "war surplus" to Orlando Brown—not Orlando Bloom—in Oakland, California. Brown intended to convert the partially sunken, rotting, dilapidated PT into a private pleasure craft. When that didn't happen, Brown put it up for sale—his asking price: $20,000. In her condition, Brown couldn't get his asking price, so he decided to donate the boat. He put the word out to PT veterans. A group in Portland said "yes" in spite of the fact that the boat was almost completely submerged under water when the vets rescued it from the California waters and moved it to Portland in 1993.

PT 658 prior to her restoration. Definitely not seaworthy.
SAVETHEPTBOATINC.COM

Over a period of 18 months, members of Save the PT Boat Inc. made 12 trips to Oakland to get the boat ready for transport to Portland. Jim Brunette recalled staying in a hotel nearby for about four days, getting up at 4 A.M. and working until late into the afternoon before heading back to the hotel. "We'd pull out the Jack Daniels and sit around until it was time to go to dinner. Then about midnight we'd hit the sack." He also remembered what an event it was when PT 658 was pulled out of the water ready for transport to Swan Island. "Some guy driving a tanker, who just happened by, saw us and stopped to inquire what we were doing. We enlisted his help—probably with a bribe of Jack Daniels—to lift PT 658 out of the water onto a barge."

Restoration of PT 658 was a major effort—a labor of love, passion, dedication, perseverance, time, energy and financial

Fourth Stop: On the Water • 171

resources. Once the word got out about restoring the boat, many people from various trades volunteered their time, including an impressive number of ex–PT boat crew members like Ken Nissan and Don Brandt who worked tirelessly to restore the boat's three original Packard engines. This was a major undertaking of the highest priority and grueling work with many setbacks. But perseverance prevailed.

In mid-September 2004, under clear skies in 70-degree weather, a majestic PT 658 cleared the dock at the Swan Island Naval Training Center at 1300 hours for her maiden voyage up the Willamette. Bob Hostetter, former PT executive officer, stood at the helm. He later turned the helm over to former PT 231 Skipper, Ed Jepsen. Also at the helm was former PT 150 Skipper, Russ Hamacheck. On board were Save the PT Boat, Inc. crew members and a few U.S. Navy visitors.

"We all loved the PT boat," remembered crew member Bob Hostetter. "The sound, the speed, the action, the small crew of only 14—2 officers and 12 enlisted men. But what really inspired us, this group of older gray-haired ex-PTers, was the challenge of seeing if PT 658 could be fully restored from a sunken mass to a fully operational PT boat. Our motto: 'Never tell an ex-PT boater it can't be done. We did it.'"

PT 658 is owned by the Naval History and Heritage Command, Washington Navy Yard, Washington, D.C.

A Bit of PT Trivia

- Motor torpedo boats like the PT-658 were used to fire torpedoes at larger ships.
- PT boat crews were nicknamed "The Mosquito Fleet."
- JFK helped make PT boats famous. He commanded PT 109.
- Sixty-nine of the 531 PT boats in service were lost during WWII.

Learn more about PT boats

Save the PT Boat, Inc. – https://www.savetheptboatinc.com

Save the PT Boat Inc. PT658 Museum on Facebook @pt658

Eyes in the Back of His Head

"COMPLIANCE IS BETTER than conviction" was a favorite saying of Lake Warden Cecil Trainer's. I met—rather I should say I interacted with—Warden Trainer on two occasions: when he gave me my boat operator's test in 1960 and then a couple of years later when he gave me a ticket for speeding on the lake after dark. His daughter Brenda and I were in the same high school class at Lake Oswego High School, but I really didn't know her very well. In fact, it's only recently when I became active with the Oswego Heritage Council that I've gotten reacquainted with Brenda and had the opportunity to learn more about the man behind the badge and the sunglasses. To me, her dad was Lake Warden Trainer—a man of the law; a Sheriff's deputy who wore a badge, packed a pistol, and patrolled the lake.

Lake warden Cecil Trainer out on patrol in Big Blackie

Having reconnected with Brenda, I knew there was more to Mr. Trainer, so I did some digging. Brenda loaned me a scrapbook with a lot of pictures, articles and artifacts saved by her mom and dad. I read through that scrapbook at least twice. Each time, I kept wishing I'd been able to meet Warden Trainer on an adult level, not kid-to-cop level, when he was working for the Lake Oswego Corporation. "Cece," as he was affectionately referred to by his friends, was considered a "jack of all trades and master of most." I was amazed to discover that behind the lawful demeanor was a man who hunted, trapped, herded sheep, and farmed. He was a scout master, musician, writer, cow puncher, and volunteer firefighter. Did I mention that he was also the head custodian at Oregon City High School?

I was totally impressed by this man's sense of volunteerism and the role safety played in his life. Cece assisted in evacuating people during the Vanport flood of 1948. He and his wife Dolora—nicknamed Skeeter—acquired, hauled, donated and delivered an old ore cart to the Oswego Iron Smelter. Mr. Trainer also took his scout troop of 30 boys to the Tillamook Burn area to help plant new trees. Does anyone even remember the "Tillamook Burn"? It was a series of catastrophic forest fires that devastated the northern Oregon Coast Range mountains 50 miles west of Portland. It began in 1933 and struck at six-year intervals through 1951, burning a combined total of 355,000 acres (554 square miles).

I had no idea what a harbinger Mr. Trainer was in the area of safety—not just boating safety, although that was one of his primary interests. He advised Gunderson Brothers and the Portland shipyard about safety issues and fire security, but his biggest influence was probably in working with the Oregon State Legislature where he introduced many safety rules that became law on any body of water in Oregon.

Oswego Lake is probably the only lake in the country to have its own set of safety rules adopted almost 100 percent as state law. Those 4 MPH signs were not just somebody's whim. They represent the authority of the state and the power of a judge to bang his gavel and demand a fine for offenders. In 1960, the Lake Corporation was given authorization by the state and the county sheriff to enforce the state boating regulations on Oswego Lake. This meant that Warden Trainer could now cite offenders directly into the district court in Oregon City. Warden Trainer was all about enforcing the rules outlined in the *Lake Oswego Corporation Handbook*.

Although Warden Trainer has passed away, he certainly left his calling card. Take a moment to think about Warden Trainer and boating safety in summer. The boating season is signaled not by the weather, but rather the rising water level of the lake.

FIFTH STOP
Oswego—Fun, Facts, Firsts

Edna Bickner (Will Bickner's wife) having fun!

"History never repeats itself, but it often rhymes."

—Mark Twain

All backdrop photos in this chapter were taken by Will Bickner.
LAKE OSWEGO PUBLIC LIBRARY DIGITAL HISTORY COLLECTION

Who's in a Name?

Although Oregon Iron and Steel (OIS) and John Corse Trullinger named many of Lake Oswego and Lake Grove streets, Truillinger never had a street named after him. He had more sensitivity to honoring historic origins when it came to names than OIS.

Athey Creek, Athey Creek Middle School: Named for pioneer James Athey who settled a donation land claim near Wankers Corners.

Bergis Road: Ellen R. Bergis was elected to city council 1954; she also delivered milk to residents in Old Town; she was a friend of Lucy Pollard, who owned a farm nearby.

Berwick Road: Named by Oswego Lake Country Club golf course architect Henry Chandler Egan after Berwick-upon-Tweed Golf Course in Goswick, England.

Bickner Street: Named for the Bickner family.

Boones Ferry Road: Named by Alphonso Boone, Daniel Boone's grandson, who came across the Oregon Trail in 1846.

Borland Road: Named after Charles G. Borland, who was an active member of the Oswego Grange. He worked for the post office and Jones Lumber Company as well as farming the 67 acres he bought from A.R. Shipley.

Bryant Road, Bryant Woods, Bryant Nature Park, Bryant Elementary School: Named for Charles W. and Mary F. Bryant, early Oswego pioneers. Bryant Elementary was built 1966, demolished in 2019, along with Waluga Junior High, to make way for the new Lakeridge Junior High campus. Unfortunately neither the historic name Waluga or Bryant were retained for the new school.

Carman Drive: Early donation land-claim pioneer family Waters and Lucretia Carman.

Chandler Road, Chandler Place: Henry Chandler Egan, designed Oswego Lake Country Club golf course.

Childs Road: Frank H. Childs, a fruit and cabbage farmer who aggressively petitioned the county to grade and lay down rock on the original dirt road, making travel easier during times of heavy rains to transport goods to Market Road (now Stafford Road).

Church Street: Most likely named by John Corse Trullinger, who, along with Albert Durham and C.W. Bryant, incorporated the first church in Oswego built at the corner of Furnace and Church Streets.

Cook Station, Cooks Butte, Shipley-Cook Farmstead: James Preston Cook, one of Oswego's earliest pioneer farming families.

Denton Way: Named for Delia "Dee" Denton, founder Festival of the Arts, first woman inducted into Royal Rosarians and Lake Oswego Rotary. Dee was a special friend. She passed away last year.

Duck Pond: Referred to as such by locals because it was nothing more than a swamp inhabited by geese, wild swans, pheasants, quail, grouse, and *ducks*. In an attempt to market their real estate holdings around the pond, Oregon Iron and Steel renamed it Lakewood Bay.

Dunthorpe: Once part of Oswego Lake Country Club district; platted and named in 1916 by Elliot R. and Alta S. Corbett of the wealthy Portland Corbett family. They had a home in Dunthorpe but it was not their first home.

Durham Road: Named for Oswego's founder Albert A. Durham and his wife Miranda.

Egan Way: Named for Oswego Lake Country Club golf course architect Henry Chandler Egan.

Elk Rock: Native Americans named the rock formation Elk Rock because they would chase elk down over the cliff, Then they would go down and get the meat for food and the hides for clothing. Located off Hwy 43 going north on the river side at Briarwood Road train trestle (Fielding and River Roads).

Fielding Road: Most probably named for Rev. Bishop Fielding Scott, who pastored at The Bishop Scott Academy.

Furnace Street: Named by OIS in honor of the first blast furnace built west of the Mississippi, in 1867.

Gans Street: Henry Gans, owned Gans Feed and Grocery which he sold to Joseph and Mary Bickner.

Glen Eagles: Named by Oswego Lake Country Club golf course architect Henry C. Egan after Gleneagles Golf Course in Scotland.

Goodall Road: Mary H. Goodall, author of *Oregon's Iron Dream*, Oswego historian and city council woman.

Goodin Easement, Goodin Station: Named for John W. Goodin, a contractor from Hillsboro (never lived in Oswego) who owned a gravel pit in the area for building roads and bridges in Lake Grove.

George Rogers Park: George Rogers, Oswego grocery merchant; also served on city council.

Green Street: Named by OIS for brothers Henry and John Green, who were business partners with H.C. Leonard. Together they owned Portland Gas Light Co. and Portland Water Co.

Hallinan School, Hallinan Road: William Hallinan, a farmer and a stone mason who worked on the furnace.

Hazelia Field: Commemorates Hazelia, Oswego's first community which encompassed the area between Rosemont and Childs Roads. Hazelia was a weed-like undergrowth which grew around trees that had to be cleared in order for land to be farmed. The Hazelia area no longer exists.

Iron Mountain Road: Named by OIS for the ore mines which were located in the hills above Iron Mountain Road and Lake Oswego Hunt.

Kirkham Street: Who it's named for is a mystery. Researchers think it most likely was named for General Ralph W. Kirkham, a director of Oswego's Oregon Iron Company. But this has never been verified.

Kruse Way: Named for the Kruse family whose farm became well-known for raising cabbage.

Ladd Street: William S. Ladd, President of OIS; Oregon's first banker—founded Ladd & Tilton Bank in Portland and Ladd and Bush Bank in Salem, which became U.S. National Bank.

Lake Grove Swim Park: Originally named Lake View Park after Lake View Villas, the housing tract owned by OIS, name changed to Lake Grove Park to reflect the name of the town of Lake Grove and Lake Grove station, stop for the Red Electric train which ran from Portland to McMinnville.

Leonard Street: Herman Camp Leonard, V.P. of Oregon Iron Company and one of its original investors. Once the fourth wealthiest man in Portland, he owned an establishment named The White House, where anything could be had. He renamed it The Riverside Hotel in 1886. It was located halfway between Portland and Oswego on Macadam Road. Owned Portland Gas and Light Co. and Portland Water Co. with Henry and John Green.

McVey Avenue: Arthur "Red" McVey, first volunteer fireman, citizen activist, janitor at Oswego School.

Macadam Avenue: Named after a Scottish inventor who created the process of macadamizing roads—a surface made by compacting broken stones even in size then binding them with tar; first macadam road in Oregon; started in 1853; completed in 1858.

Mossy Brae: A subdivision created by Alexander Pattulo located off Stafford Road just south of Johnson Road. Name reflects the cool, natural environs of the area.

Mountain Park streets: Developer Carl M. Halvorson chose names by grouping the streets according to themes—Shakespearean characters (Falstaff, Touchstone, Hotspur), composers (Gershwin, Sibelius, Bartok), artists (El Greco, Botticelli, Bantok, da Vinci), and great philosophers and writers (Cervantes, Aquinas, Erasmus).

Oswego: From the Iroquois word meaning mouth of the river or pouring out of.

Patton Road: Named for early settler Matthew Patton who purchased a portion of the Collard donation land claim for the purpose of strip mining ore from the iron mine.

Pattulo Way: Named for Alexander Pattulo, secretary of Oregon Iron and Steel and superintendent of the cement plant; family also had a donation land claim which is where he developed the Mossy Brae area (Mossy Brae Street). Both streets are off Stafford Road just south of Childs Road, not part of Oswego but they've been included because of their historical significance.

Pilkington Road: John B. Pilkington owned a large nursery where he grew fruit trees and ornamental plants, mostly roses.

Prestwick Road: Named by Oswego Lake Country Club golf course architect Henry Chandler Egan for the Prestwick Golf Club in Scotland.

Reese Road: Mr. and Mrs. Henry T. Reese donated property for Lake Grove Presbyterian Church; she dug the first shovelful of soil for the cornerstone in 1920.

Ryan Nature Park: Beth Salway Ryan, *Lake Oswego Review* photojournalist 1949–1968.

Rosemont Road: Started out as an old Indian footpath—at the time, the only trail leading west from the river at Linn City to Tuality Plains, often used by early settlers, explorers, and trappers as well as Native Americans. As wagon wheels and the hooves of oxen began to travel over the trail, it gradually widened. Ferries connected other settlements to each other along the river. Among those who traveled Rosemont: Joe Meek, a poll-taxer for the territory; Stephen Meek, who regularly drove an eight-ox team into the Tuality Plains for grain; and Oregon's most famous "Indian agent," Joe Palmer. The only proof that Rosemont Road is in its original location is that the mill stones from the old weighing station were discovered. These stones are buried beneath the driveway at 3300 Rosemont Road.

Schukart Lane: Named for Lake Oswego property developer; civic activist and philanthropist Ann Schukart. She made significant contributions to Lakewood Center for the Arts and Tryon Creek State Natural Area.

Springbrook Schools 1, 2: Named for the spring that ran alongside the building at Wembley and Twin Fir Roads.

Stafford Road: Named by a prominent Portland pioneer George A. Steel, after his hometown of Stafford, Ohio—about three hours away from where the Wankers and the Cooks came from in Ohio.

Sundeleaf Plaza, Sundeleaf Drive: Richard Sundeleaf, well-known architect who designed many Lake Oswego homes and buildings—Lake Theater building, Headlee Building across from Lake Theater, Wizer building (redeveloped as The Windward), the Cabanas.

Troon Road: Named by Oswego Lake Country Club golf course architect Henry C. Egan for Royal Troon Golf Course in Scotland.

Trullinger: Never had a street named after him as influential as he was, but he should have.

Tryon Creek State Natural Area: Socrates H. Tryon, Sr., the pioneer physician who settled the donation land claim on which the park is located.

Twin Fir: Named for the giant fir with two trunks that stood in the middle of the road.

Waluga Drive, Waluga Park: Native American word which, when spoken, sounds like the noise swans make.

Wankers Corners: Named after the Wanker family who built a store and tavern at the intersection of Stafford and Borland Roads.

Warren Court: Named for the Fred Warren family who owned three acres of land off Lakeview Blvd. Daughters Sue and Janis attended Lake Oswego High School with the author, who also resided at 17199 Warren Court for 26 years.

Westward Ho Road: The town of Westward Ho in England where the Royal North Devon Golf Club is located; named by Oswego Lake Country Club golf course architect Henry C. Egan.

Wilbur Street: Named by OIS for George D. Wilbur, who supervised the construction of the first blast furnace. He was hired by OIS for $1,200 a year.

Whitten Lane: Sarah and Richard Whitten, who filed a donation land claim in the Hazelia area in 1852.

Yates Street: Named for the Yates family; Frederick P. Morey—son of Parker Morey for whom Glenmorrie is named—was Herbert Edward Yates' uncle.

Lake Oswego Firsts

Lucia Bliss, Lake Oswego's first paid librarian, wrote the following list of Oswego's firsts in 1944. In "The Foundation: Early History of Oswego, Oregon," she wrote, "wherever possible dates and facts have been checked with accessible records. Many of the items, however, were given me by early settlers or their descendants so accuracy is questionable." Accuracy might be off, but the list is fun to peruse.

First settlers here were A.A. Durham, Nancy and Jesse Bullock, Waters and Lucretia Carman, Franklin A. Collard, Josiah and Sarah Franklin, Socrates H. Tryon, Marshall Perrin, Gabriel Walling, They came from New York, Ohio, and Iowa.

First municipal building: City Hall on A Ave., constructed in 1926

First couple to marry: Lucretia and Waters Carman

First newspaper: *Oswego Iron Worker*, printed in 1894

First church: United Methodist (became Lake Oswego United Methodist Church) organized in 1854

Although Lucia Bliss' list is short, she inspired me. There had to be more. The more I researched, the more I found. I even found a few Bliss wrote about in her manuscript but didn't put on her list. To date, I have discovered 30 more.

The first post office was established in December 1853, making it one of Oregon's oldest and one of seven in Clackamas County formed before 1855.

Oswego's first postmaster was Wesley Hull. He would advertise that mail was available for pickup in the *Oregon Spectator* newspaper.

Charlotte Calkins became **Lake Oswego's first postmistress** in 1836.

Lake Oswego's first mayor was Jerome Thomas, elected in 1910. He is buried In Oswego Pioneer Cemetery.

Henry Koehler was **Oswego's first city reccorder.**

Fifth Stop: Oswego—Fun, Facts, Firsts

Charles N. Haines was **Oswego's first marshal** in 1910. He owned a store that sold assorted goods such as BonTon Confections and also housed a laundry service and bath house.

Lucretia and Waters Carman were **the first couple to wed in Oswego,** in September 1853. He was 58. Their home at 3811 Carmen Drive was one of the first to have running water.

The first telephone in town was installed in 1910 by Herbert Lechter Nelson who owned the boat rental business at the east end of the lake and installed the telephone in order to take rental reservations.

Florence S. Dickinson, founder of Dickinson Jams and Jellies, was **the first woman to talk on the Bell telephone system.**

The first pipe foundry west of St. Louis, built by Oregon Iron and Steel to fabricate 45-inch cast iron pipe, was in Oswego. The cast iron pipes replaced hollowed-out logs used to carry water.

Among the **first ski boats on the lake** were those belonging to Ralph Coan and Dean Vincent in the 1940s. Coan named his boat *Zoomer.*

Theresa Truchot's **first issue of *The Honk*,** a newsletter she wrote for servicemen—and women—from Oswego, was published September 29, 1942. Walter Durham, Jr., remembers, because his great grandfather Albert Alonzo Durham had placed an ad on the front page advertising lumber from his sawmill.

The first diamond saw manufacturer and designer in the U.S. was Gordon Clinefelter of Oswego.

Jesse Coon was **Oswego's first rural mail carrier** from 1905 to 1910. He delivered mail using a horse-drawn buggy with a wooden box mounted on it to hold the mail.

Oregon's first nurseryman was Henderson Luelling (1809–1878). Known as the Johnny Appleseed of the West, Luelling was considered the father of Oregon's nursery industry because he introduced varietal fruit trees to Oregon and California. Seth, his brother, introduced the Bing cherry, named after orchard foreman Ah Bing.

The foursome of Willa Worthington, Ray Morris, Diane Spencer, and Don Smith—along with Leon Bullier, a Portland developer—were some of **the first to waterski on Oswego Lake** in the 1940s. Willa went on to waterski competitively and became the National Women's Waterski Champion. (Dot connection: Leon Bullier was Ralph Coan's neighbor to the east. He often entertained movie stars at his home. The one this author met was Yul Brenner. Bullier could often be seen in the winter time waterskiing in a fur coat. The infamous Stan Terry talked my Mom into waterskiing in a fur coat one New Years Day.)

Willa Worthington was **the first to master the backward swan on water skis and the first to ski over a jump backwards.**

Oswego's first public school, built in 1893, Oswego Public School was demolished 35 years later to make way for a new school. The new school, built in 1928, became Lakewood School

Mrs. Baker, **first woman to vote in an election.**

The first people to own cars in Oswego were J.R. Irving (not J.R. Ewing)—a Lozier—and the Shepherds in Glenmorrie.

Mary Scarborough Young was **the first to purchase a home site on the lake** from Ladd Estate Company in 1931—an eight-acre site known as Twin Points.

The first Girl Scout Troop in Oswego was Trillium Troop #15, established about 1927–28. Its leader was Thelma Thompson.

Mrs. H.T. Reese dug **the first shovelful of dirt for Lake Grove Presbyterian Church** in 1929.

George Rogers Park was **Lake Owego's first community park.**

Dr. Socrates H. Tryon was **the first physician licensed in Oregon.**

Dr. Rositer was **one of first doctors to come to Oswego.**

Macadam Avenue was **the first macadamized road in Oregon.** Macadamization is the process of layering stones of all the same size over dirt, then using tar as an adhesive.

The first dairy in Oswego was owned by Donald Meyer's grandfather. It was located on 3rd Street between A and B Avenues where Graham's Book and Stationery was located.

Charles "Peanuts" Didzun had **the first gas pump** and **first auto store in Oswego.**

The offspring of Virginia and Joseph Bickner, Sr.—five sons and two daughters—formed **Oswego's first orchestra.**

George W. Prosser was **the first person from the area to be elected to the state legislature.**

General Nathan Farragut Twining was **the first Air Force officer to be appointed Chief of Staff of the U.S.**

George L. Curry, president of Tualatin River Navigation and Mining, **dug the first shovelful of dirt for the Oswego Canal.**

First cabin cruiser on Lake Oswego, called the *Lake Oswego,* was owned by Paul C. Murphy and his son.

Lake Oswego's first large apartment building was constructed in 1947 at the southwest corner of Middlecrest and State Streets.

Oswego became **Oregon's first iron town** about 1860.

SIXTH STOP
Through History We Connect

Author connects with long-time Oswego resident Elva Myers (left), who worked for Douglas Aircraft as a "Rosie the Riveter" on B-17s during WWII.

AUTHOR'S CONNECTION

"History knits a community."
—anonymous

HistoryConnection Red Carpet Club

Nancy Dunis curates this group of like-minded history lovers.

HistoryConnection **Red Carpet Club** is a subscription-based informal community of folks who are passionate about local history.

This is a work in progress. Some of the ideas Nancy has in mind are...

- *HistoryConnection* Red Carpet Club pass entitling subscriber to earn points toward free History Soup Press books.

- *HistoryConnection* newzine delivered quarterly via email to your inbox featuring exclusive historical content not seen elsewhere. For a sample issue, send an email request to: nancy@thehistoricconnection.com.

- "Blathering Gatherings" at local historic venues to share, connect, reconnect, and dive deeper into historical topics.

- Red Carpet access to members-only section of website.

- Discount on History Soup Press books (Nancy's publishing company), custom webinars, NancyTalks.

Members encouraged to submit ideas and suggestions to: nancy@thehistoricconnection.com.

Author leading a tour of Heritage Rose Garden at Oswego Heritage House & Museum.
AUTHOR'S COLLECTION

Connect with Nancy

Subscribe to *The HistoriConnection* newzine:
nancy@thehistoricconnection.com

Facebook: @ History Connections – Oregon
https://www.facebook.com/groups/313402209556547/
Please, no communication via FB messenger.

Visit my website: https://www.thehistoricconnection.com

LUNCH STOP
Gazpacho Soup Recipe

"... my second most favorite soup." —Nancy

IF YOU READ *STORY SOUP*, you know my all-time favorite soup is Muligatawney, an inspiration from east Indian cuisine made with curry, apples, chicken and white wine. Perfect for cold weather, but since I am writing this during the summer, I wanted to share something cooler on the palate and easier to make. Here's my adapted and re-adpated Gazpacho recipe:

- 2 C. low sodium V-8 juice (can use tomato juice but I find that doesn't give the soup enough kick)
- 1 28-oz. can stewed or roasted tomatoes
- ½ C. chopped carrots (baby carrots are easier to cut; or use shredded)
- ½ C. chopped celery
- 1 diced cucumber (English cukes have a milder flavor and don't repeat on you)
- 1 orange or yellow pepper, chopped
- 2 cloves garlic or 2 Tbsp. minced from jar
- 1 medium zucchini, chopped (optional: throw it in if you have one that's starting to turn a bit soft)
- 1 red or walla walla onion (your choice), chopped
- 2 Tbsp. chopped chives
- 2 Tbsp. chopped parsley
- ¼ C. olive oil
- 1 Tbsp. lemon juice
- Dashes of Tabasco to taste

Throw everything in blender and whirr.... *That's it!* Well, almost. I like food with texture, so I leave the mixture a bit chunky, but you can blend until smooth if you like. Let sit in refrigerator for at least an hour (preferably two) before serving. Best if refrigerated overnight. Serve with homemade croutons* and *lots* of cilantro. I often serve this with a dollop of plain yogurt.

*To make croutons, cut store-bought garlic bread into cubes and sauté until lightly toasted. Add a little more butter to the pan so all sides are coated, and don't cube the bread pieces too small. The bigger the better.

LAST STOP
Resources and Credits

"Ideas, written ideas, are special. They are the way we transmit our stories and our ideas from one generation to the next. If we lose them, we lose our shared history. We lose much of what makes us human."

—Anonymous

Resources

Printed Matter

Fulton, Ann. *Iron, Wood, and Water: An Illustrated History of Lake Oswego.* Oregon Heritage Council, 2002.

Goodall, Mary. *Oregon's Iron Dream: A story of old Oswego and the proposed iron empire of the West.* Binfords & Mort, 1958.

Kuo, Susanna Campbell. *A Brief History of the Oregon Iron Industry* (Lake Oswego Preservation Society, 2016). https://lakeoswegopreservationsociety.org/pdf/furnace-historMar-2016_web.pdf

Kuo, Susanna Campbell, Ed. *Diary of Will Pomeroy: A Boy's Life in 1883 Oswego, Oregon.* Lake Oswego Public Library, 2018.

Lynch, Vera Martin. *Free Land for Free Men: A Story of Clackamas County.* Artline Print, 1973.

Truchot, Theresa. Lake Oswego Public Library, *In Their Own Words: A Collection of Reminiscences of Early Oswego, Oregon,* 2nd edition. 2010 (originally published 1976).

Online Resources

City of Lake Oswego, Historic Resources Advisory Board (HRAB)

- Landmark Designation List: https://www.ci.oswego.or.us/planning/landmark-designation-list
- Cultural Resources Inventory Form: https://www.ci.oswego.or.us/sites/default/files/fileattachments/boc_hrab/webpage/18342/murphy.pdf
- Historic Resource Survey Form, Oregon Inventory of Historic Properties: https://www.ci.oswego.or.us/sites/default/files/fileattachments/boc_hrab/webpage/18342/126_398_10th_street_ils.pdf

Clackamas County Family History Center
   https://www.clackamasfamilyhistory.com/

Lake Oswego Newspaper Index, *Lake Oswego Review*
https://www.ci.oswego.or.us/loreview/

Lake Oswego Public Library (LOPL) Digital History Collection
http://history.ci.oswego.or.us/

Laurelhurst Neighborhood Association, Laurelhurst History
https://www.laurelhurstpdx.org/history

Oregon Historical Society, *Oregon Encyclopedia* (online):
- Colver, Marylou. "Ladd Estate Company"
- Colver, Marylou. "William Sargent Ladd"
- Orloff, Chet, "Olmsted Portland Park Plan"

Oregon Iron Chronicles (historic newspaper articles archive)
https://www.oregonironchronicles.com

Quilt Barn Trail
https://tualatinvalley.org/local-favorites/tours-routes-trails/quilt-barn-trail/

Quilt Index, *Oregon Quilt Project* (a project of the Willamette Heritage Center in Salem)
https://quiltindex.org/view/?type=docprojects&kid=40-73-1

University of Oregon Libraries, *Historic Oregon Newspapers*
https://oregonnews.uoregon.edu/

Other Resources

Oregon Historical Society Research Library

Oswego Heritage Council collection, Journals 1993–1997

About the Author

My interest in history started with a refrigerator—Dr. William Cane's refrigerator—the one my brother bought at his estate sale in 1996. That's when the bug bit and I've been scratching the itch ever since. I've always enjoyed writing, mostly research papers when I was in college; but I did write a bit in high school. That didn't go well. My attempts to write funny weren't funny. At least not then.

When I joined the Oswego Heritage Council board, Mary Puskas announced that the *Lake Oswego Review* was interested in having someone write a short column about Lake Oswego history. Without thinking twice, I told her I would do it. I was a bit nervous because previously Dr. Stephen Beckham had been writing such a column; but I plunged ahead, developing quite a following in five years. *History Soup,* my second book, is an anthology of those articles.

Lake Oswego has been my home for over 50 years. I'm proud to say I'm a native. I attended Lakewood and Forest Hills Elementary Schools, Lake Oswego Junior High, and graduated from Lake Oswego High School. Retired from an event planning business I founded, I'm an active writer, community volunteer, and history enthusiast. "I get really excited discovering and sharing stories about Lake Oswego's past, especially stories about people, places and events no one knows much about."

When not doing volunteer work, I enjoy live theater, ballroom dancing, ice skating—via TV only these days—reading a good book and creating in the kitchen. I graduated from the University of Oregon with a BA in French and an MA in education with a psychology minor. I continue to discover new His-storioes and Her-stories to write about and share. "

Through history we connect.

—Nancy Dunis

Index

A

Abernethy Bridge 100
A.E. Doyle architectural firm 63
Alaskan Air Command 156
Albertsons 98
Allied air forces 155
Alpha Phi Fraternity 153
American Association of University Women 153
American Home 153
American Waterski Association 167
Anderson, Asbury 29
Anderson, Nellie 29
Angelou, Maya 11
architecture
   Arts and Crafts style 90
   Classic Revival style 63
   Colonial Revival style 63
   Minimal Traditional style 57
   Victorian style 62, 65
Arlington National Cemetery 157
Astoria, Oregon 147–148
Athey, James 179
Auer, John 154

B

Bailey, Barbara 108
Bailey, Van Evera 90
Bain, Freda 14
Baker, Lyle Arthur 78
Baker, Mrs. 187
Baldock Freeway Bridge 25
Banks, Bill 119–120
Barber, Gretchen 55
Barnes, Caleb 17, 18
Bartnik, Bonnie Hagen 68
Beadle, Rob 108
Becker, Jan Newton 59
Becker, Ken 94
Beck, Joan 44

Beck, Lucille (Lu) 69–71
Belluschi, Pietro 48
Benson, Agda 15
Benson Hotel 127
Bergeron, George 110
Bergis, Ellen R. 179
Bethke, Herman 20
Beth Ryan Nature Preserve 143
Better Flowers 153
Bickner Brothers 13–16
Bickner, Charles 13, 15
Bickner, Edna 177
Bickner family 179, 188
Bickner, Henry B. 13
Bickner, John 13, 15, 58, 96
Bickner, Joseph, Jr. 13, 15
Bickner, Joseph W., Sr. 13, 14, 181
Bickner, Lillian 13, 15–16
Bickner, Mary A. 13–14, 16, 62, 65, 181
Bickner's Grocery 96
Bickner, Victoria 13–14
Bickner, William E. 13, 15, 177–178
Binford and Mort Publishing 154
Binford, Peter 154
Bing, Ah 160, 186
Bird Watching in the West (book) 154
Bishop Scott Academy 180
Bliss, Lucia Bethke 5, 9, 20–22, 46, 64–65, 185
Blizzard, Bill 113
Bloedorn, Patrick 98
The Bob Shop 114
Boettcher, Charles 97
Boggs, Lilburn 24
Bonneville, Oregon 100
Boone, Alphonso 179
Boone, Alphonso, Jr. 24–25
Boone, Alphonso, Sr. 23–24
Boone Bridge 23, 25

Boone, Chloe 25
Boone, Daniel 23, 179
Boone, Jesse 23
Boone, Jesse Bryan 23
Boones Ferry Landing 23–24
Boones Ferry Park 25
Borland, Charles G. 179
Borland family 116
Bradshaw, Diane 66
Brandt, Don 172
Brenner, Yul 187
Bridgeport Village 127
Browne, Mark 106
Brownleewe, Gerhardina (Dena) 137
Brown, Orlando 171
Brumbaugh, P.M. 119
Brunette, Jim 171
Bryant, Alta 26, 29
Bryant, Charles P. 26
Bryant, Charles Wesley 26–29, 179, 180
Bryant, Cordelia 26
Bryant Elementary School 29–32, 179
　mosaic wall art 30
　teachers 30
Bryant, Ella C. 26
Bryant, Hale D. 26
Bryant, Lee 26, 29
Bryant, Mary 26, 28–29
Bryant, Mary Fay 26, 29, 179
Bryant Meresse, Mabel 28
Bryant, Myra 26
Bryant Nature Park 29
Bryant Station 29
Bryant, Vesper 26, 29
Bryant Woods 28–29
Buffalo Soldiers 61
Bullier, Leon 187
Bullock family 116
Bullock, Jesse 111–112, 137, 160, 185
Bullock, Lucy 112, 137
Bullock, Nancy Howard 111–112, 137, 185
Bull Run River 87

Burdick, Kenny 107
Butchart, Robert Pim 97–98

C

Calkins, Charlotte 132, 185
Caltech 124
Campbell, Herald 105, 110
Canby, Oregon 21
Cane, Dr. William H. 33–36, 104, 198
Cane, Winifred 33, 104
Carl's Market 68
Carman, Etta 54
Carman House 28
Carman, Lucretia 28, 179, 185–186
Carman, Waters 28, 54, 179, 185–186
Carneita 52
Carr, Phyllis 108
Cavanaugh, Helen Marie 28
Chambers, Kenton 72
Champoeg, Oregon 23
Chaney, G.E. 78
Chapel by the Lake mortuary 98
Charcoal Wagon Boy (book) 107
Chehalem Valley 122
Chemeketa Community College 150
Cheney, G.E. 59
Childs, Frank H. 180
The China Post 144
Christian Science Monitor 153
Christianson, Maynard 108
Christie School for Girls 111, 158
Chung (Shipley servant) 38
Citizens of Lake Oswego Committee 26
City Beautiful movement 90
Clackamas Community College 143
Clackamas County 41, 185
　Library 21
Clackamas, Oregon 20, 21
Clackamas Tribe 7
Clinefelter, Gordon 186
Clinefelter, Lester 132
Coan, Ralph 186, 187
Coffee, Harry 52

Colfax Landing 147
Collard, Felix 83
Collard, Franklin A. 185
Collins, Eli 121
Collins, Joe 115
Columbia River 100, 121–122
Columbia River: The Astoria Odyssey (book) 145
Colver, Marylou 197
Common Sense (magazine) 80
Community Club 34
Concord grapes 38
Congregational Church 15
Cook, Bill 54
Cook family 184
Cooking Up Oswego Memories Cookbook 94
Cook, James 40, 113
Cook, James Preston 37, 39, 40, 180
Cook, Rick xii, 40, 42, 43
Cook, Sara Ethel 40
Cooks Butte 38, 41, 65
Cook Station 39
Cook, Susie 113
Cook, Susie B. 39
Cook, Willa Worthington McGuire. *See* Willa Worthington
Cook, William 58, 77
Cook, William, Jr. 40
Cook, William, Sr. 39, 40
Coon, Jesse 132–133, 186
Cooper, Neal 77
Corbett, Elliot R. and Alta S. 180
Corvallis, Oregon 124
Cottage Hill 132
Council Bluff 9
Crazy Man's Island 9, 51
Cross, Mary Bywaters 44
Curry, George Law 25, 188
Cypress Gardens, Florida 167–168

D

Dahl restaurant 98
Dallas, Oregon 97
Davidson, C. 119
Davidson, Edgar 58, 77
Davidson, Lucien 133
DeBauw, Arsenius 62
DeBellis, Rocky 77–78, 119
DeBoer, Brent 29
Dena Rebekah Lodge 15
Denton, Dee xii
Denton, Delia "Dee" 180
Diamond Head 8–9
Diary of Will Pomeroy, The (book) 55
Dickinson, Florence S. 186
Didzun, Charles "Peanuts" 188
Dietz, Steve 60–61, 115
donation land claim
  Brown 18
  Bryant 18, 26
  Bullock 83, 111, 137
  Carman 18
  Draper 18
  Prosser 18, 134
  Shipley 65
  Walling 83, 158
Donation Land Claim Act 134
Dougan, Luther Lee 63
Dream Ride Builders xvi
Duck Pond 103, 180
Duis' police dog 109
Dundee 39
Dunis, Stuart 118–120
Dunthorpe 90
Durham, Albert Alonzo 27, 101, 145–146, 148, 180, 185–186
Durham, Miranda 180
Durham, Oregon 127
Durham, Walter, Jr. 27, 29, 186
Dyer family 116

E

Eastham, Clara 87
Eastham, Edward Lawson 86–87
Egan, Henry Chandler 179, 180, 181, 183, 184
Eisenhower, Dwight 156
Elk Rock 180

Elliot, Ian 116
Emery House 65
Emmons Grocery 138
Emmott, James Peter 114
Ertz and Burns 52
Ertz, Charles 90, 104
Estacada 21
Eugene Norton: A Tale of the Sagebrush Land (book) 81
Eugene Wine Cellar 40
Evans, Eloise 66
Evans, H.T. 65
Everett, Washington 91

F

Fairchild, Muir 156
Family Circle 151
Farmer, Don 58, 77
Farmer, Edna 108
Feather River 24
Feelin' Fine: Bill Hanley's Book (book) 81
First Addition 9, 115, 134–135
First Methodist Church 39
Fisher, L. 119
Foothills 97–98
Ford, Gerald 95
Forest Hills Elementary School 69, 107
Forest Hills, Oregon 90
Fort Vancouver 122
The Foundation: Early History of Oswego, Oregon 9, 22, 46, 64, 185
Franklin High School 144
Franklin, Josiah and Sarah 185
Freepons family 116
Friends of Tryon Creek 69, 70, 71
  Kitchen Counter Drive 69
Fulton Park 84
Funk Seed Company 28

G

Gans, Henry 13, 181
General William E. Mitchell Memorial Award 157
Gerber, Bill 110
Gere family quilts 44–45
Germond, Henry 145
Gilbert, Diane 53
Girod, Mrs. Stan 68
Gladstone, Oregon 64
Glenmorrie 82–85, 152, 187
Glenn Jackson Bridge 100
God Lights A Candle (book) 81
Gonty, Edmond 129, 130, 131
Gonty, Edward 130
Gonty, Mary 130, 131
Goodall, Ken 47
Goodall, Mary Holmes 9, 18, 22, 46–50, 75, 107–110, 181
Goodall Oil Company 47
Good Housekeeping 80
Goodin, John W. 181
Gould, Aaron 63
Government Camp, Oregon 136
Gower, John 84
Graef Circle 165, 166
Graham's Book and Stationery 187
Grange Hall 14, 15, 18, 20, 65, 135
Grant, Jerome 108
Green, Henry and John 181–182
Grigg, Helen 130
Grigg, Wally and Helen 128
Gunderson Brothers 175
"Gus the Bus" xiv

H

Haines, Charles N. 186
Hallinan family 116
Hallinan, William 181
Halvorson, Carl M. 52, 119, 182
Halvorson Island 9, 52
Hamacheck, Russ 172
Hanley, Bill 81
Hansen, Harry 93

Harding, Sally 108
Harney County 81
Hawley, Dodd and Company 135
Hazel Fern Farm 91–92
Hazelia 37, 54, 181, 184
Hazelia School 65
Headlee, Bill 105, 110
Headlee, Nancy 115
Heads Up Stylists 14
Hearts & Gizzards (quilt pattern) 42
Hemenway, Roscoe 90
Henderson, John 60
Henderson, S. 119
Hewlett, Palmer A. 31
Higgins Industries Boatworks, New Orleans 170
Hines, Harvey 26
HistoriConnection (newzine) 3
History Connection (column) xii, xiv, 1–3, 7, 35
HistoryConnection Red Carpet Club 3, 190
Holford, William G. 91
Holt, Rinehart and Winston 157
Horticulture 153
Hostetter, Bob 172
House Beautiful 151
Hoyt Arboretum 85
Hudson's Bay Company 17
Hughes, Earl 77
Hull, Wesley 132, 185
Hussman-McKeel 140

I

Imperial Flowers 14
Instenes, Jerry 115, 116
International Rose Test Garden 49
In Their Own Words (book) 27, 54, 55, 62, 77, 88, 107, 109, 119, 129, 196
Iron Mine Farm 89
Iron Mountain 104, 122
Iroquois 182
Irving farmhouse 109, 110
Irving, J.R. 187

J

Jackson, Glenn 70
Jamison, James W. 31
Jantzen Bridge 51
Jantzen, Carl 51, 52
Jantzen Island 9, 51
Jantzen Knitting Mills 51–52
Jaresche family farm 160
Jarisch, Marie 15
J. Bickner & Sons 13, 15
J.B. Pilkington Nursery 126–128
Jennings Lodge 7, 64
Jepsen, Ed 172
JFK 173
John Day, Oregon 150
Johnson, Clifford "Happy" 132–133
Johnson Creek 160
Joint Chiefs of Staff 156
Jones, Candee Clark 7
Jones Lumber Company 179
Jottings from 5th & G (group) 1
Journal of Visual Impairment and Blindness 154
Junior Historical Society 108

K

Kah/Nee/Ta Vacation Resort 150
Keith, Nathanial S. 117
Kellogg, John 102
Kennedy, Sean xv
Kent, George 34
Kingkade, Edna 15
Kirkham, Ralph W. 181
Knight Drug Company 49
Knight, Edith 49
Knight, Florence 49
Knight, Richard and Marian 48, 49
Koehler, Henry 185
Koehler's Blacksmith Shop 77
Kohorst, Kristin Z. 29
Kronquist, Shirley and Bob 142
Kruse family 54, 181
Kuo, Susanna Campbell 196
Kyle, Nellie 130

L

Lackland Air Force Base 157
Ladd Estate Company 34, 51, 89, 91, 104, 163, 165, 187, 197
　Forest Hills Branch Office 104
Ladd's Addition 92
Ladd & Tilton Bank 113
Ladd, William M. 89
Ladd, William Sargent 89, 91–92, 113, 182, 197
Ladies Home Journal 80
Lake Eloise 167
Lake Grove 18–19, 55, 57, 109, 165–166, 182
Lake Grove Presbyterian Church 187
Lake Grove School 53–56, 66
Lake Grove Swim Park 166, 182
Lake Oswego (boat) 188
Lake Oswego Chamber of Commerce 110
Lake Oswego City Council 47–48, 50, 59
Lake Oswego, City of 113
Lake Oswego Community Players 68
Lake Oswego Corporation 117–118, 176
Lake Oswego Country Club 149
Lake Oswego Country Club District 163
Lake Oswego Fire Department 40, 54, 57–59, 77, 141
Lake Oswego High School 56, 140
Lake Oswego Historic Resources Advisory Board 104
Lake Oswego Hunt Club 60–61, 134, 149, 181
Lake Oswego Junior Historical Society 50
Lake Oswego Public Library
　Beth Ryan Collection 142
　Digital History Collection 106, 197
　early history 21–22
Lake Oswego Review iii, x, xiv, 1, 2, 29, 33, 98, 113, 142, 144, 183, 197
Lake Oswego Rotary Club 110
Lake Oswego School District x, 22, 56, 166
Lake Oswego United Methodist Church 185
Lake Oswego Water Festival 169
Lakeridge Junior High x
Lakeridge Junior High School 179
Lakeridge Middle School 26
Lake View Park 165–166
Lake View Villas 165, 182
Lakewood Bay 103, 180
Lakewood Center for the Arts 63, 65, 68, 135, 183
Lakewood School 62, 63, 65–68, 77–78, 187
Lakewood Theatre Company 63, 66
Landers, Robert 107
Larsen, Rose 93
Laurelhurst Company 91
Laurelhurst Neighborhood Association 197
Laurelhurst (Portland) 92
Laurelhurst (Seattle) 91
Lawrence, Ellis F. 91
Leaves From Family Trees (book) 144
Leonard, Herman Camp 181–182
Lewis and Clark 7, 80
Lewis & Clark College
　Aubrey Watzek Award 71
Libby, Lizzie 64
Lighting Specialties 139
Lime, Oregon 98
Limited Test Ban Treaty 125
Lincoln High School 56
Linn City 9, 17
Linville, Nancy 24
Lions Club 142
Livermore, Mrs. C. Gordon 28
Lloyd Center 49
Locey, Ann 64
Lombardo, Ben 133
Long, Harold 66
The Lotus (boat) 165
Lower Cascades 122
Lucille's 14

205

Luelling, Henderson 159, 160, 186
Luelling, Seth 160, 186
Lumby, Leonard 140
Lynch, Vera Martin 196

M

Marchael Foch grapes 40
Marier, Louis 92
Market Road 9, 111
Marx, Julia 67
Mary Cullen's Kitchen (column) 46, 50
Marylhurst 83–84, 111, 158, 161
Mays, Carolyn 35
Mazamas 71
McCarty, M. 119
McCurrys (Grace and Leola) 54
McKays Grocery 139
McKeel, Elmo 139
McLaughlin, Joseph R. 91
McLoughlin, John 17
McMinnville, Oregon 182
McPherson, Clarence (a.k.a. John Buhl) 60–61
McVey, Arthur "Red" 58–59, 67, 77–79, 182
McVey Bridge 118
Mead, Frank F. 91
Meek, Joe 183
Meek, Stephen 183
Methodist Episcopal Church 67–68, 112
Meyer, Donald 187
Meyers, Bill and Robert 54
Michigan State University 43
Millbrae, California 127
Miller, George 58, 77
Miller, Rick and Erica 52
Milwaukie, Oregon 160
Miro, Gus 140
Miska, Pamela 108
Miska, Phyllis 107, 108, 110
Missoula floods 120
Moll, Lois 142
Monroe, Anne Shannon 80–81
Monroe, Rev. Andrew 81
Montavilla Sewing Center 42
Montgomery, Bob 77
Moore, Robert 17
Morey, Frederick 82
Morey Landing 84
Morey, Parker Farnsworth 82–88
Morning Oregonian 97
Morris, Ray 187
"Mosquito Fleet" 173
Mossy Brae 183
Mountain Park shopping center 109, 110, 119, 150
Mt. Bachelor Ski Area 150
Mt. Hood 104, 136
Mt. Hood Road (Highway 26) 136
Murphy, Mae Fuller 91
Murphy, Paul Cole 34, 89–92, 104, 163, 165–166, 188
  Murphy Building 104
Murphy, Paul Fuller 91
Myers, Elva 189

N

National Federation of Press Women 143
National Register of Historic Places 92
National Society of New England Women 153
Native Americans 7–9, 23, 38, 105, 122, 180, 182, 183
Natural Heritage Program 72
Naval History and Heritage Command 172
Needham, Charles 79
Nelson, Agnes 54
Nelson, Herbert Lechter 55, 186
Nelson, Mary 55
Nelson, Pat 66
Nelson, Trista 35
Newell, Cliff 142
Newlands, Lawrence 98
Newton, Grandpa 93, 95, 96
Newton, Jan 93–96

Newton, Maxine 93–94, 96
Newton, Oran "Newt" 93–95
Newton's 24 Flavors 93–96
Newton, Tom 93–96
New Town (*See also,* First Addition) 13, 79, 134, 135
Nibley, C.W. 97
Nichols, Don 169
Nissan, Ken 172
Nobel Peace Prize 125
North Pacific Rural Spirit 158
Novakofski, Lynn 168

O

Oak Grove 64
Odd Fellows 39–40, 112, , 135, 137
  Cemetery 108, 112
"Old Jimmy" (vehicle) 59
Old Town 64, 77-78, 129, 135, 179
Olmsted, Frederick Law Jr. 90
Olmsted, John Charles 90
Olmsted Portland Park Plan 197
Onward (steamship) 102, 147
Orbeck, Arvid 149–151
Orbeck Design 149–151
Orbeck, Shirley 149–150
Order of the Eastern Star, Waluga Chapter 15
Oregon Agricultural College 124
Oregon Centennial Aqua Center 169
Oregon City Enterprise 144
Oregon City Falls 100
Oregon City High School 175
Oregon City, Oregon 7, 17, 21, 86, 100, 133, 158
Oregon Coast Range 175
Oregon Department of Agriculture 73
Oregon Electric Railway 23
Oregon Falls Electric Company 86
Oregon Farmer 158
Oregon Historical Society 136, 197
Oregonian, The 46, 49, 136, 147, 153, 167, 168
Oregon Independent Grocer 139, 140

Oregon Inventory of Historic Properties 104
Oregon Iron and Steel (OIS) 18, 55, 89, 91, 97, 102, 112–113, 117, 121–122, 134, 135, 145, 165–166, 179–180, 183, 186
Oregon Iron Chronicles (archive) 197
Oregon Iron Company 135, 181–182
Oregon Iron Works 122
Oregon Journal, The 46, 47, 50, 153
Oregon Legislature 137
Oregon Parks Foundation 71
Oregon Portland Cement Company 97, 98, 99
Oregon Presswomen 143
Oregon Quilt Project 43, 44
Oregon Rare and Endangered Plant Project 71–73
Oregon's Iron Dream (book) 9, 18, 22, 46, 47, 50, 54, 181, 196
Oregon Spectator 132, 185
Oregon State Historic Preservation Office 41
Oregon State Legislature 148, 175
Oregon State University (OSU) 39, 49, 93, 124
  Herbarium 71–72
Oregon Territory 132
Oregon Trail 23, 159, 179
Orloff, Chet 197
Oswego Auto Parts 133
Oswego Canal 101–103, 188
Oswego Chamber of Commerce 34
Oswego Country Store 133
Oswego Creek 83, 134
Oswego Fire Department 40
Oswego Grammar School 63, 65
Oswego Grange No. 175 38–39
Oswego Heritage Council iii, 35, 105, 110, 174, 197–198
  Historic Home Tour 41, 57
Oswego Heritage House and Museum xiii, 34, 94, 96, 104, 105–106, 145
Oswego Hydro 117, 119
Oswego Iron Smelter 175

Oswego Iron Worker 185
Oswego Lake 18, 51, 89, 103, 117–118, 176
Oswego Lake Country Club golf course 134, 179, 180, 181, 183, 184
Oswego Lake Country Club District 89, 90
Oswego Landing 102
Oswego Library Association 21
Oswego Milling Company 146–147
Oswego Nursery 159
Oswego Pioneer Cemetery 111–115, 131, 133, 137, 144, 185
Oswego Public School 14, 62, 65, 77, 78, 182, 187
Oswego School District No. 47 64, 137
Oswego State Bank 15
Oswego Women's Club 21
Owego Pipe Foundry 18
Oyalla, Bill 105

P

Palisades district 90
Palmer, Joe 183
Papulski, Pete 67
Parker, Jamison 90
Parsons School of Design 149
Patton, Catherine Grimes 121–123
Patton, Matthew 121–123, 182
Pattonsburg, Missouri 121
Pattulo, Alexander 182–183
Pauling, Ava Helen Miller 113, 124–125
Pauling, Charles 113
Pauling, Linus 100, 113, 124–125
Peg Tree 132
Pendergrass, Bill 140
Penttila, Bryan 145
People's Transportation Company 146
Perrin, Marshall 185
Phantom Bluff 9
Phoenix, Oregon 61
Pilkington, Clarke 126–127, 128

Pilkington, Esther 126, 128
Pilkington, John B., Jr. ("Dad") 126–128
Pilkington, John B., Sr. 126, 159, 183
PIlkington, Nellie 128
Pipes, Wade 90
Platt, Hayley C. 29
Platts, Ben and Rocky 54
Pollard, Johanna 130
Pollard, Lucy 129–131, 179
Pollard (Puylaert), Peter 129
Pomeroy, James 55
Pomeroy, Will 55
Pope, Dick, Sr. 167–168
Pope, Julie 167
Portland 9, 21, 23, 39, 63, 80, 86, 90, 98, 100, 101, 111, 121, 126, 136, 139, 160, 171, 175, 182
Portland Art Museum 151
Portland Cement Company (*See also*, Oregon Portland Cement Company) 97
Portland City Council 49
Portland Gas and Light Co. 182
Portland General Electric (PGE) 87
Portland Hydraulic Elevator Company 86
Portland Police Bureau 33
Portland Realty Board 92
Portland shipyard 175
Portland State University 150–151
Portland Water Company 87, 182
Portland Water Spectacular 168
Powers Brothers Dairy 84
Prosser, Dena 136
Prosser, George T. 137
Prosser, George W. 17, 58, 77, 112, 115, 132–137, 188
Prosser, Henry 134
Prosser, Lucy E. 132–133
Prosser, Mary 134–135
Prosser Mine 104, 134
Prosser, Susan 136–137
Prosser, Sylver 112, 136–137
PT 658 (boat) 170–173

Puskas, Mary iii
Puylaert, Felicie Marie Virginie.
   See Pollard, Lucy

Q
Quilt Barn Trail Project of
   Washington County 42, 197
Quilt Index Project 42, 43, 44, 197

R
Raleigh Hills 128
Rathbun, Jim xii, 138, 140–141
Reaksecker, Fred 61
Red Electric 19, 165, 182
Redwork (quilt pattern) 44
Reed, Simeon G. 92
Reese, Henry T. 183
Reese, Mrs. H.T. 187
Remsen, Bill 139, 140
Remsen, Chet 138–140
Remsen, Evelyn 138–140
Remsen, Jim 140
Remsen's Lakeside Thriftway 139–140
Remsen's Market and Grocery 138
Risley Landing 64
Riverdale district 90
Riverside Hotel 182
River View Cemetery 28–29, 113
Riverwood district 90
Robin's Nest 17
Rogers, George 67, 126, 169, 181
Rogers Park 104, 135, 169, 187
Roseburg, Oregon 97
Rose, F. 119
Rositer, Dr. 187
Ruby, Will xvi
Rufus, Oregon 97
Ryan, Cornelius 144
Ryan, Elizabeth Salway (Beth)
   142–144, 183

S
Sacred Heart Cemetery 113, 129, 137
Safeway 13, 15, 48, 93, 141
   mosaic mural 149–150
Salem, Oregon 23, 28, 43
Samuelson, Ralph 167
Santee, Richard 114–115
Saturday Evening Post 80
Save the PT Boat, Inc. 171–173
Schaeffer, C, 119
Schaubel, Ethel 113–116
Schollander, Don 169
Schollander, Mrs. Wendell 169
Schukart, Ann 51, 183
Scott, Rev. Bishop Fielding 180
Seattle, Washington 91
Seed, Soil, and Science (book) 28
Sequoia, giant 48, 50
Shannon, George 80
Shepherd family 187
Shipley, Adam Randolph (A.R.)
   37–39, 65, 113, 179
Shipley, Alphonso Wood 37
Shipley, Celinda E. Himes 37, 113
Shipley-Cook Farmstead 38–42, 65
Shipley, Cora 37
Shipley family 116
Shipley, Lester 37
Shipley, Macinda 37
Shipley, Milton 37
Shipley, Randolph Chaplain 37
Shoalwater Bay 122
Shon-Tay office building 109
Siddall, Jean 69–73
Singing in the Rain (book) 81
Sisters of St. Mary's 31
Smith, David 60
Smith, Don 187
Smith, Gene 109
Smith, Ward C. 55
Snider, Pat 142
Sons of Neptune 51
South Oswego Addition 123
Sparks from Home Fires (book) 81

Spencer, Bill 169
Spencer, Diane 169, 187
Spencer, Sharon 169
Sposito, Sam 139
Springbrook School (1, 2 & 3) 54–55, 65–66, 183
Stafford 111
Stafford School 20, 65
Stanford University 70, 126, 127
Steel, George A. 111, 184
Stein, Gary iii, xi, xii
St. Mary's Academy for Girls 160
Stone, John 54
Story Soup (book) 1, 2
Strachan, Mary 22
Strong, Frederick H. 89, 91
Strong, Mary 109
Stubblefield, Jerry 52
Sucker Creek 101, 117, 122, 158
Sucker Lake and Tualatin River Railroad 146–147
Sucker Lake (*See also,* Oswego Lake) 101–103, 117, 147
Sundeleaf, Emma 52
Sundeleaf, Richard 52, 57, 90, 184
Sunny Hill 142, 144
Sun Portland Cement Company 98
Sunset 153
Swan Island 170
Swan Island Coast Guard and Naval Reserve 170–172

T

Tate, Tim and Nadeen 14
Terry, Stan 187
Thacker, Gertrude 107–108
The Dalles, Oregon 121, 150
The Honk (newsletter) 186
The Nature Conservancy 71–72
Theta Sigma (now Women in Communication), Portland Chapter 143
Thomas Frazer Hazelwood Farm 92
Thomas, Jerome 185
Thomas Kay Woolen Mill 43

Thompson, Thelma 187
Thompson, Tommy 52
Thurlow, Dorothy 7, 9
Tillamook Burn 175
Tim's Germs 14
Trainer, Brenda 174
Trainer, Cecil 119, 174–176
Trainer, Dolora "Skeeter" 175
Trillium Girl Scout Troop #15 187
Truchot, Theresa 46–47, 62, 77–79, 88, 107–110, 119, 129, 186, 196
Trullinger, Hannah Boyles 146–147
Trullinger, John Corse 102, 145–148, 180
Tryon Creek 69
   State Natural Area 70, 183, 184
Tryon, Frances 134
Tryon, Socrates H. 134, 184–185, 187
Tualatin River 9, 26, 37, 101–102, 118
Tualatin River Navigation and Manufacturing Co. (TRNM) 101
   Chinese laborers from 102
Tualatin Valley 101, 146
Tualatin Valley Builders Supply 53
Tuality Plains 183
Tuality Tribe 23
Twain, Mark 177
Twin Fir 184
Twining, Captain Robert G. 156
Twining, Charles 152–153
Twining, Clarence 152
Twining, Ed 153
Twining, Frances Staver 152–154
Twining, General Nathan Farragut v, 155–157, 188
Twining, Maude McKeever 156–157
Twining, Nathan A. 156
Twining, Olivia B. 156
Twin Points 187

U

Undine (boat) 122
United States Electric Lighting Company 86–87

University of Oregon 144, 197
  Distinguished Service Award 71
Uplands Elementary 108
U.S. Air Force 155–156
U.S. Army 155
U.S. Army Corps of Engineers 149
U.S. Naval Academy 155
U.S. Navy 172

V

Van Bibber, Chloe 23
Vancouver, Washington 100
Vanport flood of 1948 175
Villa Maria 160, 161
Vincent, Dean 186
Vintage Tour Bus Company xvii
Vrilakas, Sue 72

W

Walla Walla, Washington 86
Walling, Adam 158–159
Walling, Albert G. 158–159
Walling family 116
Walling, Francis 158
Walling, Gabriel 185
Walling, George Washington 158–160
Walling, Lucy and Gabriel 158
Waluga 5, 32, 184
Waluga Junior High School 26, 179
Wanker family 116, 184
Warner, Bill iii, xii, 110
Warner Hall 66
Warren, Fred, family 184
Washington High School 63
Washington Park 49
Watson, Esther 136
Watts, John 66
Waverly Country Club 160
Wayne Corporation xvi
Wayne Works xvi
Western Homes and Gardens 153
Westinghouse turbine 118
West Linn 17, 94, 100, 126
West Linn High School 56

West Point 155
Wetherell, H.M. 65
The White House 182
Whitehouse, Morris 90
White, Virgil 66
Whitten, Sarah and Richard 184
Wilbur, George D. 184
Willamette Falls 7, 102, 146
Willamette Heritage Center 43
Willamette Nursery 158
Willamette River 7, 9, 20, 23, 25–26, 64, 82, 87, 97, 98, 101, 117, 152, 158, 160, 172
Willamette Tribe 38
Willamette Valley 23, 27–28, 41, 122, 160
Williams, Esther 168
Wilmot, Wilbur 54
Wilsonville, Oregon 23, 25
Wing, E. 119
Wooley, Ivan M. 136
Worthington family 54, 116
Worthington, Nina 114
Worthington, Willa 167–169, 187
Wright, Frank Lloyd 63
WWII 170, 173, 189

Y

Yakima, Washington 80
Yates, Herbert Edward 83, 88
Young, Mary Scarborough 126, 187

Z

Zika, Brittany 30
Zimmerman, Edith 53
Zion Lutheran Church 48
Zoomer (boat) 186

Made in the USA
Columbia, SC
25 May 2023